ITIL® V3 Guide to Software Asset Management

London: TSO

Published by TSO (The Stationery Office) and available from:

Online
www.tsoshop.co.uk

Mail, Telephone, Fax & E-mail
TSO
PO Box 29, Norwich, NR3 1GN
Telephone orders/General enquiries: 0870 600 5522
Fax orders: 0870 600 5533
E-mail: customer.services@tso.co.uk
Textphone 0870 240 3701

TSO@Blackwell and other Accredited Agents

First published 2009
Third impression 2014
ISBN 978 0 11 331106 4

Printed in the United Kingdom for The Stationery Office,
Material is FSC certified. Sourced from responsible sources.

P002429128   c3.5   05/11

Contents

List of figures   vi

List of tables   vii

Preface   viii

Acknowledgements   ix

1   Introduction   1

  1.1   ITIL   3

  1.2   What is SAM?   4

  1.3   The need for SAM   4

  1.4   SAM principles   5

  1.5   Benefits   7

  1.6   The possible problems   10

  1.7   Costs   12

  1.8   Implementation approaches   13

  1.9   Minimum implementation recommendations   14

  1.10   World-class SAM   16

  1.11   How SAM maps to ITIL   16

  1.12   How this guide is organized   20

2   Context   21

  2.1   Special characteristics of software assets   23

  2.2   Legal context   24

  2.3   Software industry supply chain   26

  2.4   Other software industry players   28

3   Making the business case   29

  3.1   Develop a vision and strategy   31

  3.2   Investigate the issues   33

  3.3   Document the business case   34

  3.4   Sell the business case   35

4   Organization, roles and responsibilities   37

  4.1   Decision about centralization   39

  4.2   Centralization or decentralization of SAM databases   40

  4.3   Respective roles of procurement management and ICT management   41

  4.4   Roles and responsibilities   41

5   Process overview   45

  5.1   Overall management processes   48

  5.2   Core asset management processes   49

  5.3   Logistics processes   51

  5.4   Verification and compliance processes   60

  5.5   Relationship management processes   63

  5.6   Special situations   65

6   Implementation overview   67

  6.1   Preparation   69

  6.2   Getting there   70

  6.3   Staying there   72

  6.4   Proving you are staying there   72

7 Tools and technology 75

7.1 Asset inventory tools 79

7.2 Discovery tools 79

7.3 Metering tools 80

7.4 Licence management tools 81

7.5 Contract management tools 82

7.6 Demand management tools 82

7.7 Deployment management tools 82

7.8 Security tools 82

7.9 Procurement tools 82

7.10 Vendor licence management technology 83

8 Partners and software asset management 85

8.1 SAM guidance materials 87

8.2 SAM consultancy 88

8.3 Outsourcing of SAM functions 88

8.4 Audits 89

8.5 Certification 89

8.6 Conferences and workshops 90

8.7 Licensing advice 91

8.8 Historical purchase records and effective licensing 91

8.9 Current purchase records 92

8.10 Directories and assessments of SAM tools 93

8.11 SAM tools 93

8.12 Implementation assistance for SAM tools 93

8.13 Special considerations for reseller relationships 93

9 Mapping SAM to ITIL and other approaches 95

9.1 SAM and ITIL 97

9.2 SAM and ISO/IEC 20000 101

9.3 SAM and ISO/IEC 19770 103

9.4 SAM and COBIT 104

9.5 SAM and other management frameworks and guidelines 107

Appendix A Software licensing overview 109

A.1 When licences are required 111

A.2 Basic types of licence 112

A.3 Types of licences by sales channel 114

A.4 Counterfeits 115

A.5 What is 'proof of licence'? 116

A.6 Physical management of software licences 117

A.7 Other common licensing problems 119

Appendix B Considerations in selecting SAM tools 121

B.1 General points of consideration 123

B.2 Practical guidelines for the selection of SAM tools 124

Appendix C Possible SAM database contents 127

C.1 Software licence inventory 129

C.2 Installed software inventory 133

C.3 Source documentation 134

C.4 Working documentation 135

C.5 Media 136

C.6 Guidance documentation 136

C.7 Hardware inventory 136

Appendix D   Choosing a SAM partner   137

Appendix E   The detailed contents of a SAM business case   143

Appendix F   Example contents of a software policy   147

    F.1   Sample policy on the use of hardware and software   149

    F.2   Acknowledgement of hardware/ software policy   150

Further information   151

Abbreviations and glossary   155

    Abbreviations   157

    Glossary   158

Index   169

List of figures

Figure 1.1   The principles of SAM

Figure 1.2   Relationship between SAM and the ITIL framework

Figure 1.3   The structure of this guide

Figure 2.1   The software industry supply chain

Figure 5.1   SAM process areas

Figure 5.2   The application lifecycle

Figure 5.3   The modified application lifecycle (including externally sourced software)

Figure 5.4   The SAM procurement process

Figure 5.5   Checking receipt of manufacturer proof of licence

Figure 5.6   SAM verification and compliance processes

Figure 6.1   SAM implementation

Figure 7.1   SAM technology architecture

Figure 9.1   ITIL use of the DML and CMS

Figure 9.2   Relationship between SAM and the ISO/IEC 20000 service management processes

Figure 9.3   The ISO/IEC 19770 SAM processes

Figure 9.4   The COBIT framework

List of tables

Table 1.1   NAO and generic recommendations
            for purchasing and managing
            software licences

Table C.1   Licence information and inventory

Table C.2   Inventory of installed software

Table C.3   Filing of source documentation

Table C.4   Filing of working documentation

Table D.1   Importance criteria for potential
            SAM partners

Preface

The ethos behind the development of ITIL (information technology infrastructure library) is the recognition that organizations are increasingly dependent upon IT to satisfy their corporate aims and meet their business needs. This growing dependency leads to a bigger demand for quality IT services – quality that is matched to business needs and user requirements as they emerge. ITIL provides the guidance that will help to match that quality against needs and costs in order to provide the best IT match for the business.

This is true no matter what the type or size of organization, be it national government, a multinational conglomerate, a decentralized office with either a local or centralized IT provision, an outsourced service provider, or a single office environment with one person providing IT support. In each case, there is the requirement to provide an economical service that is reliable, consistent and fit for purpose.

Infrastructure management is concerned with the processes, organization and tools to provide a stable IT and communication infrastructure, and is the foundation for ITIL service management processes, promoting a quality approach to achieving business effectiveness and efficiency in the use of information systems. ITIL service management processes are intended to be implemented so that they underpin but do not dictate the business processes of an organization. IT service providers will be striving to improve the quality of the service, but at the same time they will be trying to reduce the costs or, as a minimum, maintain costs at the current level.

For each of the management processes described in this publication, one or more roles have been identified for carrying out the activities and producing the deliverables associated with the process. It should be recognized that it is often possible to allocate more than one role to an individual. Conversely, in larger organizations, more than one individual may be required to fulfil a role. The purpose of a role, as described here, is to locate responsibility, not to suggest an organization structure.

Acknowledgements

Guidance was distilled from the experience of a range of people working in software asset management (SAM), IT service management and/or ICT infrastructure management.

Colin Rudd, Director of IT Enterprise Management Systems Ltd (ITEMS), was the lead author for this publication. Colin has worked in the IT industry for more than 40 years. He has been heavily involved in the development of ITIL, authoring or contributing to the production modules in every version released. Recently, Colin was the lead author for *Service Design* (TSO, 2007) in the latest version of ITIL. He was recognized in 2002 by the IT Service Management Forum (itSMF), which is the ITIL service management user forum, with the presentation of its lifetime achievement award for his work in the area of IT service management.

The project was managed by **David Bicket**, senior manager at Deloitte and Touche. David also contributed extensively to the design and writing. Further contributions were made by **Steve Rudd** of IT Enterprise Management Services Ltd.

TSO (The Stationery Office) would like to thank itSMF for its help in the quality assurance of this publication. TSO would also like to thank the following people who have generously contributed their time to reviewing the content of this publication:

Tristan Boot	University of Canterbury
Steven Davison	Infrasolve
Stephen Griffiths	Whitmore Solutions Ltd
Steven Heal	KPMG LLP
David Jones	Pink Elephant EMEA Ltd
Tricia Lewin	Matwin Management Services Ltd
Steven Russman	The International Business Software Managers Association
John A. Sowerby	DHL IT Services
Dean Taylor	VEGA Consulting Services Ltd

The objective of the review exercise was to update the original book in line with the core ITIL version 3 publications, COBIT® version 4.1 and the ISO/IEC 20000 service management international standard.

Thanks are still due to all of those who contributed to and reviewed the original software asset management book as this new edition represents an update rather than a rewrite of the original content. These people include:

Richard Best	Teksys Ltd
Wolfgang Bösing	Siemens Information & Communications Networks Manager
Richard Bull	
Brian Davies	Barclays Bank PLC
Paul Diamond	Director
Jenny Dugmore	ConnectSphere
Ronald B. Falciani	IBM Corporation
Shaun Fröhlich	Teksys Ltd
David Gilchrist	Systems Management International
Barry Joyce	Hewlett Packard
Ronda Kiser	Whirlpool
Shirley Lacy	ConnectSphere
Eamonn McDonough	Department of Transport
Denise E. Mason	Xansa
David Nicoll	WPP

Paul Noonan	Bytes Technology Group
M. J. Perry	Vantico
David Phillips	Microsoft UK
Marianne Rinde	Hewlett Packard
Marina Schröder	Aspera OHG
Vaughan Smith	Microsoft UK
David Ward	IBM United Kingdom Ltd

Organizations listed above were correct when the original publication, *Software Asset Management* (TSO, 2003), was published.

Introduction 1

1 Introduction

Most organizations today are dependent for their continued operation upon information technology (IT) or information and communications technologies (ICT) as it is increasingly being called. Software is one of the most critical elements of ICT and most organizations make huge investments in software, whether internally developed or externally procured. However, organizations often do not invest commensurate effort into managing these software assets.

This guide has been developed to assist with understanding what software asset management (SAM) is, and to explain what is required to perform it effectively and efficiently as identified in industry 'best practice'. These guidelines can be tailored to fit any organization, regardless of size.

This guide should be of interest to anybody involved in the acquisition, development, operation, use or retirement of software within an organization. It should be of particular interest to two types of individual:

- Directors and other members of senior management with corporate governance responsibility, including responsibility for software assets and the risks associated with them. These individuals will be most concerned with this introductory chapter
- Individuals responsible for investigating or implementing improved processes and systems for SAM. These individuals should be interested in the entire guide.

1.1 ITIL

This guide is complementary to the core ITIL publications (*Service Strategy, Service Design, Service Transition, Service Operation* and *Continual Service Improvement*, TSO, 2007) and is intended to be consistent with all of its principles and processes. ITIL is the most widely accepted approach to IT service management in the world, providing a comprehensive and consistent set of best practices for IT service management. This promotes a quality approach to achieving business effectiveness and efficiency in the use of information systems.

The ITIL framework is owned by the Office of Government Commerce (OGC) of the UK government, and was initially developed to provide guidance to UK government departments. It has subsequently achieved acceptance worldwide, and a number of software manufacturers' own methodologies are aligned with it. It is fast becoming a de facto standard used by some of the world's leading businesses. An international standard (ISO/IEC 20000) has also been developed that has close links with ITIL. This guide is closely aligned with ISO/IEC 20000 and with the ISO 9000 quality standard. More recently, an international software asset management standard ISO/IEC 19770 was produced, aligned with ISO/IEC 20000, and largely based on the content within this publication.

This guide may be used by organizations that are already committed to ITIL best-practice approaches in all areas, and also by organizations that are adopting such guidance on a more limited basis. If this is the first ITIL guide to be used within an organization, then it is strongly recommended that more is learnt about the full range of guidance available from ITIL (see www.itil.co.uk and also the related user group website at www.itsmf.com).

Software asset management is part of overall IT service management, and must be understood in this context. The SAM database, for example, is logically part of the configuration management system (CMS) that supports all of IT service management. These interrelationships between SAM and all of IT service management as defined by ITIL are explained in section 1.11 and, in more detail, in Chapter 9. There is also repeated reference to other service management areas throughout this guide. The terminology used in this guide is consistent, to the extent practical, with terminology throughout the rest of ITIL, while also retaining consistency with software industry terminology.

1.2 WHAT IS SAM?

Software asset management means different things to different people. The definition used within this guide is as set out in the box.

> **Definition**
>
> Software asset management (SAM) is all of the infrastructure and processes necessary for the effective management, control and protection of the software assets within an organization, throughout all stages of their lifecycle.

SAM does not include hardware asset management, which will not be covered within this guide except for those aspects that are necessary for effective SAM (collectively, software asset management and hardware asset management can be referred to as IT asset management, or ITAM.) More information on hardware asset management can be found in the service asset and configuration management section of *Service Transition* (TSO, 2007). Generally speaking, however, SAM is more complex and more demanding than hardware asset management and therefore the SAM processes need to be greater in scope and more comprehensive in content. As a result, systems that can handle SAM can usually be expected to handle hardware asset management as well. Furthermore, it must be stressed that it is essential for hardware assets to be managed as well as software assets, even though hardware assets are not covered here.

The coverage in this guide is intended to be manufacturer- and platform-neutral, to provide impartial practical guidance. Specific products are not mentioned, nor is there focus on specific architectures such as mainframe or client/server. Most of the coverage should be equally applicable to PC workstations as to servers and mainframes, and even to network communications equipment such as routers.

1.3 THE NEED FOR SAM

The underlying justification for SAM is the need to apply good corporate governance to an organization's software assets. These typically include much of an organization's asset base, are critical to its continued operations, and underlie some of an organization's main legal and contractual obligations. This is a common-sense justification, but it is increasingly being reinforced by statutory or regulatory corporate governance requirements, such as Turnbull in the UK and Sarbanes-Oxley in the USA. Consequently, the ultimate responsibility for good corporate governance of software assets lies with an organization's senior management, and success or failure in this area ultimately rests with them.

Key message

The importance of SAM is illustrated by a quote from George Cox, the Director General of the Institute of Directors in the UK:

'The role and importance of externally acquired software has changed dramatically in recent years, to the point now where it has to be regarded as a business asset and managed as such. Software asset management has become an imperative, not an option. Software licences are business assets. Without them directors expose their business and themselves to constraints and to legal and financial risk.'

There is also a broader justification for SAM, which is all of the benefits it helps to deliver. Further detail about these is given in section 1.5.

1.4 SAM PRINCIPLES

The overall objective of all SAM processes is that of good corporate governance – namely, the management of an organization's software assets, including the management of the risks arising from the use of those assets.

Objective

The overall objective of SAM is to manage, control and protect an organization's software assets, including management of the risks arising from the use of those software assets.

A scalable, structured approach needs to be adopted in order to achieve this for each organization. The sequencing of the events involved in this structured approach is illustrated in Figure 1.1.

The most important requirements for a SAM project are to have a clear vision and strategy that are owned by senior management. They should be the driver for initiating everything else in SAM, and in particular they drive the processes of creating the business case (see Chapter 3). The vision and strategy should include any overarching vision

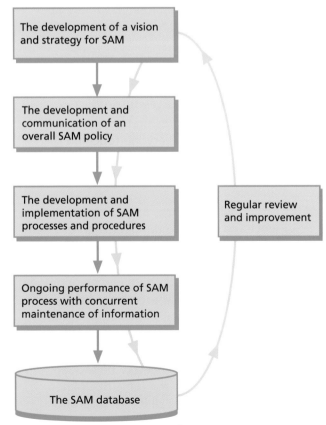

Figure 1.1 The principles of SAM

and strategy for service asset and configuration management (SACM) as a whole, i.e. for all of ICT and not limited just to SAM.

Overall policies need to be established and communicated effectively to the entire organization. Corresponding responsibilities also need to be clarified and communicated. These issues are addressed in several places throughout this guide, including in Chapter 4, section 5.1 and Appendix F.

Detailed processes need to be defined and implemented, including automated capabilities and written procedures. The majority of the content of this guide addresses this area, including, in particular, Chapters 5 and 6.

Key messages

- Board-level sponsorship and commitment are essential to ensure successful SAM
- Policies and procedures that are practical and mandatory for everyone touching IT assets (procurement to retirement) must be developed, implemented and monitored for adherence
- Effective SAM processes and inventories support and facilitate the operation of many other processes and best practice.

Once SAM is implemented, there will be ongoing performance issues of SAM processes with concurrent maintenance of information in the set of SAM databases (which are part of the configuration management system or CMS in ITIL terminology) that will need to be tackled. SAM should be subject to the same disciplines of service management as all ICT services and infrastructure, as discussed in the core ITIL publications. For example, SAM cannot continue

to function properly without attention to areas such as continuity of operations and capacity management. However, these more general topics are not discussed in detail in this guide.

The basis of any good SAM system to have is accurate and up-to-date SAM information, together with the processes for control of its accuracy. The SAM databases also provide essential information for the integration of SAM processes with other ICT and business processes. The databases should be considered logically as a single database, but may consist of several physically separate, but linked, databases. In highly decentralized organizations, each autonomous unit may have its own autonomous database, but there needs to be central collection of some data to achieve the greatest benefits of SAM. This area is discussed in more detail in Chapter 4.

There also needs to be a regular process of review and improvement affecting all areas already addressed. At one level there should be review for compliance with defined policies and procedures and, where appropriate, corrective action. There may be opportunities for improvements in efficiency and effectiveness, and definitions of responsibilities. Vision may also change, perhaps in response to changing market opportunities and threats or technological developments. These issues are briefly addressed in section 5.1, but repeating the entire process described above, at least for review purposes, is necessary periodically.

Key message

It is impossible to implement an effective SAM process without the successful design, development, implementation and maintenance of accurate SAM databases, automatically updated, wherever possible from the live infrastructure.

1.5   BENEFITS

The potential benefits of well-implemented SAM are significant and usually greatly exceed the implementation and operating costs. There are many ways of categorizing these benefits. Sections 1.5.1–1.5.4 list the most significant benefits experienced by many organizations.

1.5.1 Managing risks

SAM facilitates the management of significant business risks including:

■ **Legal and financial exposure**   There is risk to the organization if licensing terms for externally procured software are not properly observed. This exposure may arise from enforcement agencies directly (e.g. police or customs), from industry associations (e.g. Business Software Alliance [BSA] or Federation Against Software Theft [FAST]) or from software manufacturers. It may be initiated by: tip-offs from disgruntled employees (whistle blowers – potentially for financial reward); by supplier knowledge (e.g. the reseller who fails to get a contract knowing the competitor's pricing cannot include licences); by software manufacturer analyses of customer purchasing; or by 'accident' (e.g. a police sweep through an entire building requiring companies to prove their licences). The characteristics of externally acquired software assets underlie these major exposures. Further detail is given in section 2.1. In summary, the characteristics of commercial software assets underlie the following major exposures:

● software being resident/installed without licences being purchased
● loss of proof of licences which have been purchased, including licences underlying upgrades
● complex terms and conditions which may be breached unknowingly
● incorrect reliance on resellers

■ **Damaged reputation**   An organization's reputation may be damaged by the publicity that results if legal problems become publicly known. Likewise, an ICT department's reputation may be damaged within the organization and within the ICT community if it experiences major unexpected problems related to the control of software assets, e.g. licensing, roll-outs or support

■ **Unexpected financial and workload impact**   Problems related to software assets, e.g. licensing, can have significant unexpected financial impact in areas such as cash flow, which can then impact on other planned activities. Likewise, ad hoc efforts to address licensing issues in response to external events can require major unplanned amounts of time from management and operational personnel, regardless of whether there is any ultimate direct financial impact

■ **Security breaches including unauthorized disclosure of confidential information**   Security may be breached, and confidential information may be disclosed because of failure to implement adequate measures for security patch distribution

Key message

'About 95% of exploits occur after bulletins and patches are put out ... the reason the exploit is effective is because the patch uptake is too low' (Chief security strategist for a major software manufacturer).

■ **Unexpected problems with acquisitions/ mergers/demergers**   Failure to address SAM issues properly, including licensing, during 'due diligence' activity for acquisitions/mergers/ demergers can expose the organization to significant unexpected financial risk and operational impact

■ **Interruption of operations**   The problems caused by poor SAM can sometimes affect continuity of operations, e.g. shutdowns caused by legal reasons, virus infections or poorly deployed software updates. Conversely, good SAM can mitigate problems that might otherwise affect operations severely, e.g. being able to deploy security patches more quickly

■ **Unsupportable operations**   There can be a risk of certain software-dependent operations being unsupportable without good SAM. For example, there may be critical applications reliant upon unlicensed software that ceases to be available for sale, preventing the possibility of continuing to use it while becoming conformant. Likewise, software manufacturers may cease upgrade and technical support for some products. Good SAM processes and related management planning should minimize such exposures.

1.5.2 Controlling costs

Proper SAM allows for significant cost savings, not only in direct expenditure on software, but also in related process and infrastructure costs. Some specific ways in which cost control can be improved as a result of good SAM are:

■ **Better negotiating position**   Knowing with certainty that an organization is conformant with licensing terms and conditions gives it a strong negotiating position with software manufacturers. Conversely, if there is a lack of clarity about the correctness of licensing, the reseller or software manufacturer may use that uncertainty to its negotiating advantage, with the possibility of a software audit being threatened to help close a deal that may not be in the organization's best interest. Also, where there are effective SAM practices in place within an organization, there are good relationships and interfaces between procurement and operational staff ensuring that not only are the financial aspects of software acquisition well covered, but so are the functional aspects

■ **Improved strategic infrastructure planning**   Better knowledge about what is being installed/used, and better deployment capabilities, will facilitate the assessment of strategic software alternatives. For example, it is common for multinational companies to find dominant usage of one software manufacturer's products, with small pockets of competitive products that can typically be replaced under existing agreements at little or no additional cost. Alternatively, it will be easier to plan major infrastructure changes, including to competitive products

■ **Prevention of software over- deployment**   Proper SAM will help identify where software is needed, rather than just where it is installed, e.g. by monitoring active usage. A common finding is that standard configurations as installed are over-specified compared with what end-users actively use. Better identification of end-user needs can significantly reduce software and hardware requirements and costs as a result. Pull technology can allow for real-time deployment according to end-user requirements without the costs of comprehensive global deployments. Existing software investment will not be eliminated, but future costs may be greatly reduced by controlled redeployment of released licences. This information can also be important for negotiating major software agreements

■ **Reduced hardware costs** Just as proper SAM can help prevent over-deployment of software, it will also help identify over-deployment of hardware. It can also facilitate the identification of other major opportunities for hardware savings, such as server consolidation, and time-phased purchasing requirements, which can be used in some cases to negotiate significant supplier cost savings

■ **Improved software purchasing arrangements** A common finding, especially with large organizations, is that there are multiple purchasing points often making poor or no use of centrally arranged volume purchasing agreements for software. In these cases, the organization could often achieve significantly better pricing if global purchasing arrangements covered all purchases

■ **Reduced costs of internal licensing support** One of the most significant hidden costs of SAM is the cost of developing and maintaining licensing expertise among management and operational personnel, which in any case is often done inadequately with the attendant risks that result. By providing centralized skilled resources with licensing knowledge, the corresponding hidden costs at

local levels can be greatly reduced, and the risk of mistakes though lack of proper knowledge can also be minimized

■ **Reductions in process and direct infrastructure costs** There are clear savings that can be achieved in many areas as a result of good SAM implementations. For example:

● well-designed infrastructure processes, working with accurate information about software assets, will function more efficiently, e.g. for change impact assessments, roll-outs and upgrades

● organizations will have SAM costs whether they formally recognize them or not. Savings can be expected if common solutions to asset management requirements can be implemented throughout the organization instead of via independent ad hoc approaches, as is often the case

■ **Reductions in problem-resolution costs** A well-run ICT infrastructure, including proper SAM, should result in fewer operational problems with their attendant impacts, cost and otherwise. Likewise, a well-run ICT infrastructure should allow for faster and more cost-effective resolutions of those problems that do occur

■ **Potential tax benefits** Focus on tax issues, such as accelerated depreciation of some software expenditures, may result in significant tax benefits. (These may depend on many factors, such as the country, the industry and the organization's tax position.)

1.5.3 Obtaining competitive advantage

Proper SAM gives the organization competitive advantage in several major ways:

- **Better quality decision making**   More accurate data on software assets, more readily available, allows for better quality management. In particular, good SAM improves transparency in overall ICT management. For example, in a large organization with many business units which have their own ICT support structures, SAM can provide the transparency to help ensure that all ICT planning is assessed against common criteria. This can be useful in the renewal of assets, which otherwise might rely on the forcefulness of the individual ICT managers
- **Faster time to market**   Proper SAM gives the organization the ability to roll out improved ICT functionality faster but still with proper control. As a result, initiatives can be implemented more quickly, and reaction to changes in markets or competition can be faster, to give the organization competitive advantage. Conversely, poor SAM may give the competitive advantage to others
- **Faster and easier integration after mergers and acquisitions**   Having proper SAM, and the ability to implement it quickly in new units, can facilitate the integration of organizations after mergers and acquisitions. The faster the ICT integration can be achieved, the sooner the anticipated benefits of the business combination should be achieved.

1.5.4 Enhancing employee motivation and the workplace environment

Proper SAM helps combat some of the main contributors to employee dissatisfaction, namely repeated ICT problems, and excessive delays in implementing new functionality. This can be particularly important for ICT support personnel who otherwise spend considerable time 'fire-fighting' without experiencing management support for their efforts.

> **Example**
>
> A large multinational that had just completed the implementation of SAM was approached by one of its software manufacturers with the threat of a licensing audit. The chief information officer (CIO) knew exactly how much of that software manufacturer's software was being used, and where, and even knew that there was over-licensing because of changing ICT infrastructures. The CIO immediately agreed to the audit, but the software manufacturer never conducted it. The CIO's improved view of software usage allowed him to achieve significant cost savings with that software manufacturer and most other software manufacturers as well. Significant savings on planned future hardware expenditures were also achieved.

1.6   THE POSSIBLE PROBLEMS

Some of the potential problems that may arise related to SAM include the following, many of which are similar to the problems of all system initiatives, but some of which have particular relevance to SAM.

1.6.1 Conflict with decentralization culture

A common management philosophy is 'small is beautiful', with heavy reliance on decentralization to stimulate initiative and innovation. This philosophy may work in many areas, but has significant limitations in the area of SAM because many of the significant procurement benefits are achieved by centralization, and many of the related risks are best managed on a centralized basis. Conversely, decentralized ICT management approaches can create global risk for the organization because software manufacturers and legal authorities will not differentiate to suit the management approach if there are individual units that are seen as violating licensing terms and conditions. A comparison can be made with treasury functions, e.g. for capital expenditure. Even in highly decentralized organizations, this function tends to be centralized or have strong central oversight. SAM needs to be treated in a similar fashion.

1.6.2 Lack of senior management support

Successful SAM implementation is much more than the implementation of a tool. It will typically require significant culture change, which can only be achieved with active senior management support. It may be hard to get that support for a variety of reasons, e.g. SAM is not the current management fad, or SAM is not seen as being exciting. It is, instead, a 'nuts and bolts' function that underpins the successful management of software and with it the operational infrastructure of the organization. Proper senior management support will result in sufficient budget, resources, knowledge and skills being allocated to SAM implementation and ongoing operation.

1.6.3 Lack of clear responsibilities

An implementation project without clearly assigned responsibilities, both for the project and for ongoing responsibilities after implementation, will likely fail. In practice, it may be difficult to define responsibilities clearly as, for example, when there are already grey areas between group ICT and business unit ICT responsibilities, and when there are existing outsourcing agreements and service level agreements (SLAs) with responsibilities already defined or excluded.

1.6.4 Imbalance between 'customized' and 'off-the-shelf' software perspectives

There is a point of view sometimes expressed that software must always be chosen and tailored to meet an organization's unique requirements. This approach can easily be taken to unjustifiable extremes. An organization's requirements should certainly be determined before selecting software. However, if those requirements cannot easily be met using existing software packages without customization, then the requirements should be reassessed. Otherwise, there is a strong risk of software being customized to meet inflexible and poorly thought-out requirements that would result in a costly solution supplied late and which does not meet real SAM requirements. Such a solution may represent a bureaucratic and inflexible view of control. By analogy, an organization that custom-designs its accounting software to meet existing accounting procedures is normally asking for disaster. Unfortunately, the SAM tools available do not yet have the degree of maturity of current accounting and logistical systems, where most major packages provide similar and generally accepted functionality. Current 'best practice' in the SAM area is to use a combination of available tools but without extensive customization. This area will clearly continue to develop.

1.6.5 Underestimating the effort required to identify installed software

It is common to underestimate the amount of time and effort required to turn detailed discovery information into useful information about installed applications. There may be thousands of files associated with a single application or licence. Different combinations may indicate partial installs, full installs or incomplete uninstalls, and there may be different levels of updates or security patches to identify. The demands escalate if in-house and non-commercial software is included in the analysis. The tool(s) selected, and possibly the partner selected to help implement/use the tool(s), can be important in controlling time and effort in this area.

1.6.6 Legal requirements

Implementing SAM, especially for a multinational organization, may require unexpected amounts of effort to comply with local legislation. Particular consideration should be given to data protection issues (confidentiality of personal information, transmission of personal information across borders etc.). In some countries, there may also be a requirement to consult local employee organizations, e.g. a Works Council. Some types of metering, in particular, may be viewed as employee monitoring, and may need careful discussion.

1.6.7 Lack of end-user support

End-users typically will not support a new system unless they see it being actively supported by senior management, and unless they see a direct personal benefit from it. End-users need to see SAM and ICT in general as being responsive to their needs, and minimizing problems and hassle. This is especially important where users have the ability to procure, download or install software themselves.

1.6.8 Software licence variation

There are so many different types, terms and conditions of software licences that it makes it very difficult for organizations and their SAM processes to allow and adjust for the different situations and variations.

1.6.9 Lack of communication

If ICT staff and the user community are not made aware of the organization's software policy and of their roles and responsibilities with regard to the use of software assets, then the enforcement of SAM processes within an organization is difficult.

Example

A large travel organization was starting SAM implementation with adequate people and resources committed to the project. However, overall ownership was not agreed and people's roles and responsibilities within the implementation of the SAM processes were not clearly defined, documented and agreed. The result was that much time was wasted, and the project was delayed and almost cancelled due to these issues before remedial actions were taken.

Key message

Ensure that sponsorship, ownership, terms of reference, scope, processes, roles and responsibilities are clearly defined in the early stages of SAM implementation.

1.7 COSTS

The implementation of SAM will inevitably incur costs. The scale of these costs will depend in part on the implementation approach chosen (see section 1.8), and also on other factors such as:

- Size, culture and structure of the organization
- Level of senior management sponsorship and commitment to SAM within the organization
- Size, scope and timescale of the proposed project
- Current use of technology and software within the organization
- Current state and maturity of the SAM processes within the organization
- Tools to be used and the level of automation planned
- Degree to which a customized solution is wanted versus the willingness to use existing/available tools and systems that may not meet all perceived requirements (see section 1.6)
- SAM skills, resources and knowledge within the organization
- Number of devices in use, e.g. mainframe, mid-range, desktops, servers etc.

The main costs will be incurred within the following areas:

- **People** People will be required to develop and perform the roles and activities required within the SAM processes, both during their implementation and their subsequent ongoing operation. This may require the involvement of senior management, project managers, external partners and consultants where the skills, knowledge and availability of internal resources are not suitable
- **Tools** Both hardware and software may need to be selected, implemented, configured and tailored to automate aspects of the SAM processes

- **Accommodation** The costs for SAM staff and the storage costs for actual software assets and documentation
- **Interfaces** These may need to be developed, using internal or external resources
- **Corrective licences** There may be additional costs to make up for any identified shortfalls in software licences. These costs may deter an organization from starting a SAM project; however, they must be tackled and in many organizations the savings made from SAM can more than compensate for the additional costs.

Key message

The costs associated with the implementation of SAM may seem extensive, even prohibitive. However, intelligent exploitation of existing infrastructure, processes and tools should help to contain costs. A good SAM implementation should typically bring significant financial savings within a year of completion.

SAM costs should furthermore be seen as necessary expenditure to control the many software-related risks faced by an organization.

1.8 IMPLEMENTATION APPROACHES

The implementation of SAM within an organization is an extensive and demanding task. There are many different approaches that can be adopted, and these generally fall into three categories:

- **Internal project** This involves the use of resources from within an organization to implement the SAM processes. It is the preferred approach if the necessary SAM skills and knowledge are present and available within the organization. It should involve the use of an approved organizational project methodology, e.g. PRINCE2

- **Partnership project**   This involves the use of an external partner or partner(s) to assist with the implementation of SAM. This approach has distinct advantages where there is a lack of either internal skills or resources within the required SAM timescale

- **Outsourced project or managed service**   This involves contracting an external organization or partner to implement the complete activity to agreed key performance indicators (KPIs) aligned to project critical success factors (CSFs).

It is critically important if the complete activity is outsourced that the client still takes ownership of the strategy and makes decisions on information provided. Any outsourced contract should be on the basis of KPIs that require the supplier to manage effectively the assets, rather than payment based on number of assets managed. Otherwise, there is no incentive to dispose of assets not required by the business.

These approaches can be applied not only to the implementation of SAM processes but also to their continued operation.

The approach selected by an individual organization will depend upon many factors, including overall cost, the demands for 'business as usual', and the availability of budget and other required resources.

1.9   MINIMUM IMPLEMENTATION RECOMMENDATIONS

Smaller organizations, especially those ones that have not already embraced ITIL, may find the extensive coverage of this guide more than they are seeking initially. It is strongly recommended that somebody be given the responsibility for developing an appropriate SAM strategy for each organization, and that reading this entire guide should be one of the required tasks. That being said, this section summarizes the most significant recommendations that all organizations should expect to implement, regardless of size.

1.9.1   Overall baseline recommendations

The following list is the suggested minimum set of recommendations for software asset management in any size or type of organization:

- **Vision**   Senior management should determine why SAM is needed in a way that aligns with the overall organizational vision and objectives. The vision ideally should include other ITIL service areas and be aligned with other business and organizational strategies and visions (see section 3.1)

- **Decision about centralization**   Determine the degree of centralization to be required in SAM. Some of the most significant benefits of SAM come from centralization of expertise, procurement and risk management functions, regardless of the degree of decentralization of other functions. It is a similar situation to capital expenditure control (see section 4.1)

- **Responsibilities and policies**   Establish clear overall responsibilities and policies for SAM commensurate with the decision on centralization. Responsibilities should include risk management for contractual and legal risks. Policies should make clear the obligations of all officers, employees and contractors and the consequences of violations. These policies should be consistent with other policies in use within the organization (e.g. HR policies and information security policies - see sections 4.4, 5.1.3 and Appendix F)

■ **Skills and competence** Develop and maintain strong SAM skills including software licensing. Read and understand software licensing contracts, with particular focus on volume-licensing contracts that give audit rights to software manufacturers. If reliance is being placed on an outside organization, that organization must provide input into all necessary SAM processes, and not just advice on licences for new software being purchased. Remember also that legal exposures cannot be contracted out, so there must be enough internal competence to ensure adequate controls over these exposures (see section 5.1.4)

■ **Detailed strategy** Develop clear statements of detailed ICT strategy. Standardization of common software and of deployment configurations is of particular importance for overall cost reduction (additional information on strategies is contained in *Service Strategy* [TSO, 2007])

■ **Contracting** Choose appropriate partners, including those for the supply of software. Ensure that software purchasing arrangements are structured to minimize cost while still ensuring control. For example, global contracts typically give the best pricing, but reporting of usage should be at a lower level (e.g. by country, subsidiary or business unit) to facilitate reconciliations and control (see Chapter 8, section 5.5.1 and Appendix D)

■ **Procedures** Establish robust procurement, deployment and retirement procedures that ensure compliance with policies and which themselves capture necessary information and assets, especially proof of licence (see sections 5.3.4, 5.3.6 and 5.3.9)

■ **Inventories** Create and maintain accurate inventories of software and hardware assets including costs, with secure control over access to software assets, e.g. proof of licence, and distribution copies of software (see section 5.2.1 and Appendix C)

■ **Reconciliations** Perform regular reconciliations of (a) what is actually installed against (b) what is recorded against (c) licences owned (for licensed software), and resolve any identified exceptions promptly. The frequency of the reconciliations will depend on the effectiveness of procedures for accurate record-keeping and licence management, but should not be less than yearly. Some organizations do this on a continuous automated basis (see section 5.4)

■ **Cost–benefit analysis** Develop, collect and utilize relevant data for ICT procurement decision-making about total cost of ownership (TCO) including benefits, both quantified and non-quantified (see section 5.2.5).

1.9.2 National Audit Office recommendations

The Comptroller and Auditor General in the UK is the head of the National Audit Office (NAO) and reports to Parliament. He certifies the accounts of all government departments and a wide range of other public sector bodies, and can report on the economy, efficiency and effectiveness with which departments and other bodies have used their resources. He issued a report on 1 May 2003 on 'Purchasing and Managing Software Licences' (www.nao.gov.uk, report HC 579) with a number of recommendations that can be considered minimum best-procurement practice for UK government organizations. A comparable generic recommendation is made by this guide for all organizations (Table 1.1). This

Table 1.1 NAO and generic recommendations for purchasing and managing software licences

	NAO recommendations for UK government departments © UK National Audit Office	Generic recommendations for all organizations
	For departments	*For all organizations with direct purchasing responsibility for software assets*
1	Maintain reliable information to assess the extent of their expenditure on software and supporting licences	Same
2	Consider in the first instance using the Memoranda of Understanding negotiated by OGC with suppliers	Consider in the first instance centralized purchasing arrangements
3	Check regularly to ensure that no unlicensed software is being used on their systems	Same
4	Consider the total cost of ownership when purchasing major upgrades or new systems	Same
	For the Office of Government Commerce	*For group/corporate ICT procurement functions*
5	Monitor carefully take-up of the Memoranda of Understanding and the discounts received by departments	Monitor decentralized use of centralized purchasing arrangements and benefits achieved

is effectively a specialized subset of the baseline recommendations given in section 1.9.1 above.

Table 1.1 has been included as an example. Other sectors and industries may have other recommendations and guidelines based on additional regulatory and industry sector requirements.

1.10 WORLD-CLASS SAM

For those organizations that are implementing more than just the minimum, the question is how far to go. Metrics in this area are limited. However, there does appear to be at least one differentiator of what can be considered 'world-class SAM' – the types of software covered by SAM implementation. The first approach (which most organizations implement with SAM) is to provide version control and implementation confirmation (or copy control)

of 'standard' software. The second (which far fewer organizations implement successfully) covers all software including in-house applications and non-commercial software such as internet file-swapping applications. The second gives better risk management, but the first is adequate as a procurement tool.

1.11 HOW SAM MAPS TO ITIL

The relationship between SAM and the modules within ITIL is illustrated in Figure 1.2.

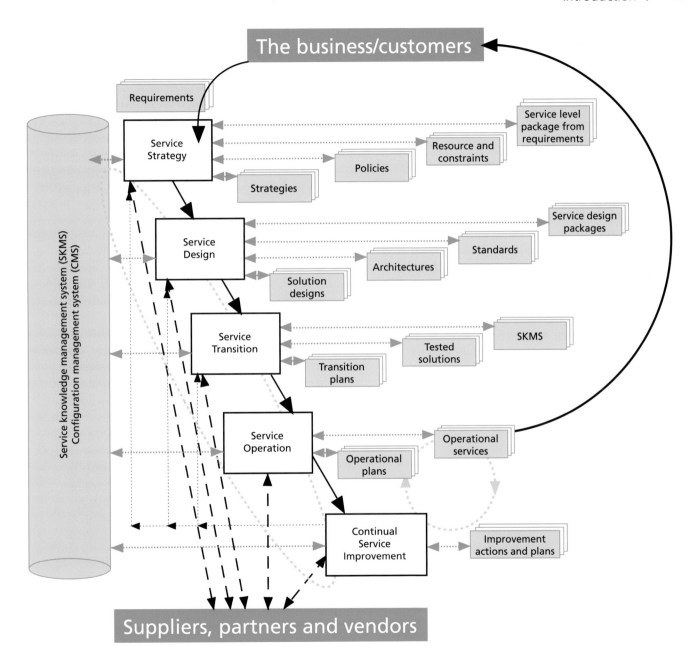

Figure 1.2 Relationship between SAM and the ITIL framework

The individual areas can be briefly described as follows:

- *Service Strategy* provides guidance on how to design, develop and implement service management, not only as an organizational capability but also as a strategic asset. Guidance is provided on the principles underpinning the practice of service management, which are useful for developing service management policies, guidelines and processes across the ITIL service lifecycle. Topics covered in *Service Strategy* include the development of markets (internal and external), service assets, service catalogue and implementation of strategy through the service lifecycle. Financial management, service portfolio management, organizational development and strategic risks are among other major topics

- *Service Design* provides guidance for the design and development of services and service management processes. It covers design principles and methods for converting strategic objectives into portfolios of services and service assets. The scope of *Service Design* is not limited to new services. It includes the changes and improvements necessary to increase or maintain value to customers over the lifecycle of services, the continuity of services, achievement of service levels and conformance to standards and regulations. It guides organizations on to develop design capabilities for service management

- *Service Transition* provides guidance for the development and improvement of capabilities for transitioning new and changed services into operations. This publication provides guidance on how the requirements of service strategy encoded in service design are effectively realized in service operations while controlling the risks of failure and disruption. The publication combines practices in release and deployment management, programme management and risk management, and places them in the practical context of service management. It provides guidance on managing the complexity related to changes to services and service management processes – preventing undesired consequences while allowing for innovation

- *Service Operation* provides guidance on achieving effectiveness and efficiency in the delivery and support of services so as to ensure value for the customer and the service provider. Strategic objectives are ultimately realized through service operations, therefore making it a critical capability. Guidance is provided on how to maintain stability in service operations, allowing for changes in design, scale, scope and service levels. Organizations are provided with detailed process guidelines, methods and tools for use in two major control perspectives: reactive and proactive. Managers and practitioners are provided with knowledge allowing them to make better decisions in areas such as managing the availability of services, controlling demand, optimizing capacity utilization, scheduling operations and fixing problems. Guidance is provided on supporting operations through new models and architectures such as shared services, utility computing, internet services and mobile commerce

- *Continual Service Improvement* provides instrumental guidance in creating and maintaining value for customers through better design, transition and operation of services. It combines principles, practices and

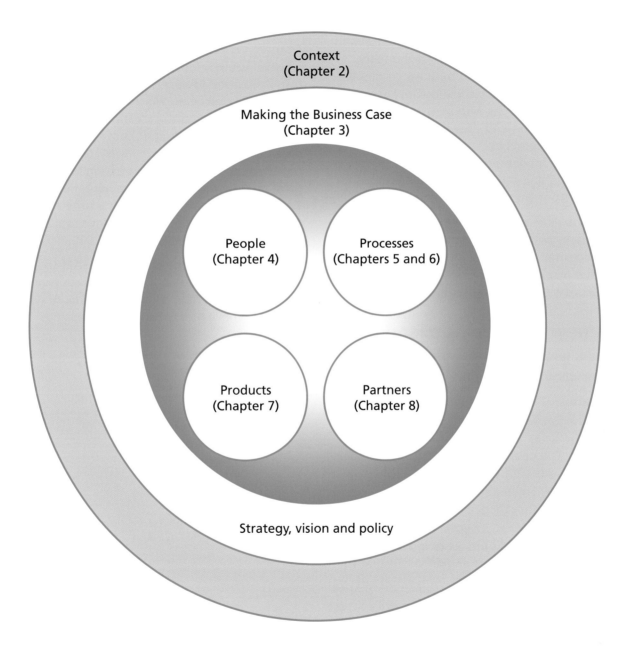

Figure 1.3 The structure of this guide

methods from quality management, change management and capability improvement. Organizations learn to realize incremental and large-scale improvements in service quality, operational efficiency and business continuity. Guidance is provided for linking improvement efforts and outcomes with service strategy, design, transition and operation. A closed-loop feedback system, based on the Plan–Do–Check–Act (PDCA) model specified in ISO/IEC 20000, is established and capable of receiving inputs for change from any planning perspective.

This section illustrates the general areas of commonality between SAM and the stages of the service lifecycle. Further detailed information about the mapping of SAM to ITIL and other approaches is given in Chapter 9.

1.12 HOW THIS GUIDE IS ORGANIZED

This guide is organized as indicated in Figure 1.3, which emphasizes the four Ps:

- **Processes** The management processes required for effective SAM (which is the emphasis of this guide)
- **People** The people involved in SAM and their roles and responsibilities
- **Products** The management technology and tools used within the SAM processes
- **Partners** The other, external organizations involved within SAM processes including manufacturers, resellers and SAM consultants.

Chapter 1 provides an overall introduction to SAM and Chapter 2 gives information about the context and the special nature of software assets. Chapter 3 provides advice on making the business case for SAM and covers the development of the vision and the strategy, with an example policy document included in Appendix F.

Chapter 4 covers some of the most important 'people' issues related to organization, roles and responsibilities. Chapters 5 and 6 give information about SAM processes, which is the main focus of the guide, including the creation and maintenance of the SAM database set. (Chapter 5 gives the details of SAM processes in live systems, including review, audit and improvement, while Chapter 6 gives an overview of the implementation.) Chapter 7 covers 'products', i.e. the tools and technology. Chapter 8 covers the types of service available from partners.

Chapter 9 explains the mapping of SAM to ITIL and similar approaches. The appendices provide supporting materials, such as Appendix A, which contains an overview of software licensing.

Context 2

2 Context

Software assets are essentially intellectual property assets. These types of asset have unique characteristics that differentiate them from the more common, purely physical assets. In order to appreciate the implications for SAM, it is useful to understand more about these unique characteristics, and about the industry that has generated the majority of software assets in use in the world today.

2.1 SPECIAL CHARACTERISTICS OF SOFTWARE ASSETS

There are many assets that ICT organizations need to manage, and software is just one of them. The major types of asset that need to be managed within ICT are:

- Computer and network equipment
- Environmental equipment
- Buildings and facilities
- Software assets
- Data and databases
- Processes and policies
- Documentation and contracts
- People.

However, software is probably the most complex to manage, because of the complexity of its lifecycle. Furthermore, commercial software can have significant legal and financial risks associated with its special characteristics.

- **Risk of software being used without licences being purchased:**
  - liability for licence payments typically can be incurred without going through a procurement process, simply by installing/using the software, even if done without proper authorization
  - even with proper authorization, software installations may not be properly reported. This is because volume-licensing contracts typically allow for installation before 'reporting', i.e. before paying for the software. Reporting is honour based, but with audit rights for the software manufacturer. Because there is no physical requirement to purchase a licence before using it, there is increased reliance on proper internal controls to ensure that reporting is correct. However, these are different from the typical controls for other areas of procurement, so there is significant risk that they will not be performed correctly
- **Risk of the loss of proof of licences which have been purchased:**
  - licences may be lost physically because the importance of proof of licence documentation is often not recognized, and therefore there may be a failure to keep them under any sort of control
  - licences may be lost 'administratively' because a central unit may perform purchasing, obtaining consolidated licences for all purchases, which are then administratively difficult to tie back to

the ordering units. Also, subsidiary units that were licensed may then be sold or reorganized, and the licences will not move with them

- licences may be ordered via a reseller, but proper proof of licence may not be received from the software manufacturer. The reporting flow for volume purchases from an end-customer to the software manufacturer is largely one way, without the usual inherent checks of physical purchases. The loop is typically closed only by the customer checking for the receipt of proper proof of licence from the software manufacturer. This is not a standard process for physical procurement processes, and consequently it may be omitted or performed poorly. As a result, proofs of licence that were paid for may never be received, and furthermore may not be recognized as missing

Risk of terms and conditions being breached unknowingly:

- externally procured software assets typically have complex legal conditions that can be misunderstood even by people working in the area
- software is frequently upgraded and licence conditions can change with upgrades
- what constitutes 'proof of licence' can be a complex issue in itself. The issues surrounding this area are explained in Appendix A

Risk of incorrect reliance on resellers:

- there is sometimes a tri-partite legal relationship between a software manufacturer, reseller and the customer that does not apply to most other assets. It is not possible to rely solely on the reseller. Each set of relationships needs to be properly managed. What a reseller says usually does not change the contractual obligations of the end-user organization towards the software manufacturer

Risk of loss of licences:

- hardware may fail or be disposed off without the software being de-installed or recovered, resulting in loss of licences.

A piece of software within the ICT environment may consist of all or some of the following components:

- The master copy of the software itself on the master media
- Distribution copies of the software on free-standing media or on servers
- The software licence certificate or other 'proof of licence'
- Terms and conditions of licence
- Support contracts
- Software pass codes or licence keys
- Software maintenance authorization codes
- The software release documentation
- Upgrade components
- The installed operational instances of the software.

The management of software would therefore need to control all of these different aspects and would involve interfacing with many other ICT asset management processes and units.

2.2 LEGAL CONTEXT

One of the main exposures with externally acquired software is the legal exposure that comes with use contrary to terms and conditions or legislation. The legal basis for this exposure depends on the country and contractual conditions, but mainly comprises:

- Copyright legislation
- Trademark legislation
- Contract law.

Violations may be unintentional or intentional. Unintentional violations are common and may be caused by various factors:

- Lack of understanding of licensing terms and conditions
- Lack of records about software usage, and often not even knowing the number of PCs in use
- Lack of robust ICT deployment procedures to ensure that all installations are properly authorized, including ensuring that necessary licences are procured
- Purchase from or installation by suppliers of unlicensed or counterfeit software.

Although such violations may be unintentional, they are still violations. Furthermore, there is usually a 'duty of care' on the part of organizations for the way they conduct their business. Failure to focus on the issue of legal risk because of other priorities is unlikely to be an acceptable excuse with software manufacturers or in court.

Directors and other senior management may take several steps to reduce personal exposure to such violations. Ensuring that there are adequate systems of internal control in operation is an important factor, and good SAM processes help meet this requirement. It is also important to ensure that employees understand relevant policies and confirm this with signed statements and that there are meaningful disciplinary measures in place for violations, in line with HR policies.

As mentioned above, the unknowing purchase from or installation by suppliers of unlicensed or counterfeit software is a major source of exposure to risk of litigation. This may occur for many reasons:

- **Lack of clarity between supplier and customer about the supply of licences** A common problem can occur when a supplier provides hardware with pre-installed software, or when a supplier provides implementation support, e.g. for a system migration. Often the end-user organization will assume that the supplier is providing the licences. The supplier, however, may assume that the customer is providing the licences, perhaps under an existing volume-licensing contract held by the customer. The customer is almost certainly responsible, unless the supplier has a clear contractual obligation to provide the licences. Even in this case, the customer has a 'duty of care' to ensure that appropriate proof of licence is received
- **Counterfeit software** There is a significant risk of receiving counterfeit software, including counterfeit media and 'proof of licence' especially with longer supply chains in which there is more opportunity for counterfeit

products to enter the chain. This topic is covered in more detail in Appendix A

- **Hard-disk loading** Hard-disk loading refers to the practice, more likely to be encountered among smaller suppliers, of putting software on customers' machines without supplying the corresponding media or licences. Often this will occur as part of the supply of hardware, e.g. on a new PC or server. Even if the software is mentioned on the invoice, this is usually not sufficient, and proper documentation of proof of licence is still required.

There are also legal issues involved with the installation of software, because of the common practice of requiring a user to agree to licence terms and conditions as part of the installation process. Users typically do not bother to read these terms and conditions. In some cases, the terms include allowing the manufacturer to install and run other programs on the user's computer, e.g. for marketing purposes.

2.3 SOFTWARE INDUSTRY SUPPLY CHAIN

The situation with regard to the sale and distribution of software is a complex one. There are many different organizations and players involved, with the user organization at the end of a long and sometimes complex chain. The onus is on the user organization to ensure that the software provided is genuine. The roles of the main players within the software industry are detailed in Figure 2.1 and below:

- **Software manufacturers/vendors/ publishers** These roles are responsible for providing quality software that is fit for purpose, together with all licensing information necessary for the operation and use of the

Examples

The scale of the issue

Over 6,500 European businesses were taken to court in a 12-month period for contravention of software copyright.

BSA studies estimate that about 25% of business software used in the UK is unlicensed.

BSA studies estimate that about 40% of business software used worldwide is unlicensed.

Recently, there have been many high-profile examples of organizations contravening copyright laws, ranging from high street retailers and international banks, through local government to small- and medium-sized businesses. The penalties for these offences have ranged from a few thousand pounds to hundreds of thousands of pounds.

A national distributor with a chain of several hundred resellers had to pay an undisclosed sum of damages for activities over a number of years where it had been inadvertently distributing counterfeit copies of illegal software that it had purchased in good faith.

A study conducted in the late 1990s in one country identified that more than twice as many PC motherboards were being supplied to the market by one hardware manufacturer alone compared with the number of operating systems purchased in total in that country.

software. Software remains the intellectual property of the manufacturer. All that is purchased by the user is a licence to use the software

- **Original equipment manufacturers (OEMs)** These install software on their hardware and sell it on as a package. The licence for OEM software is typically with the OEM, and not with the software manufacturer (the main exception to that general rule). As a result, OEM licences are usually contractually bound to the hardware they are sold with, and are not transferable to other machines

- **Distributors** These usually do not deal directly with end-customers, but only with software manufacturers and resellers. They deal in very high volumes of software of low-volume types, e.g. retail products, low-volume programs and OEM products. Some counterfeit products have entered the supply channel via (smaller) distributors

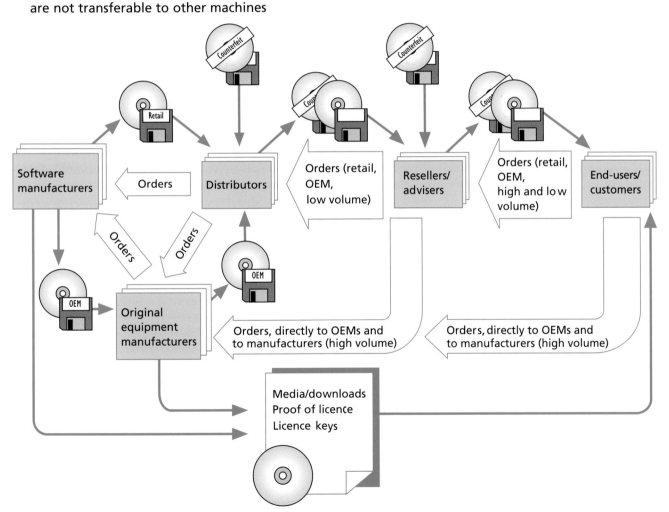

Figure 2.1 The software industry supply chain. Note that this figure is simplified. Not all channels are shown, nor all possibilities for ordering/delivering, or for the introduction of counterfeit product.

- **Resellers** These usually deal directly with end-customers, for most levels of software purchasing, e.g. retail, OEM, and low-volume and high-volume programs. Counterfeit products have entered the supply channel via resellers, more commonly via smaller resellers. Some software manufacturers have authorized resellers, with whom the risk of buying counterfeit products should be minimized

- **Advisers** These assist customers in placing orders, but the contractual relationships are directly between the customer and the software manufacturer. The software manufacturer pays a fee to the adviser. Many distributor organizations also offer advisory services

- **End-user organization** This is the organization that ultimately purchases the licences, and has ultimate responsibility for ensuring that genuine proof of licence is received for all purchases made.

2.4 OTHER SOFTWARE INDUSTRY PLAYERS

There are several other types of industry player that should also be mentioned here (see also Chapter 8).

- **Standards and professional organizations** These provide professional guidance on the development and control of software and related services. Examples include:
  - ITIL – see the preface to this guide for further explanation
  - International Organization for Standardization (ISO) – the owner of ISO/IEC 19770, the SAM standard
  - ISO – the owner of ISO/IEC 20000, the IT service management standard, and other associated standards

- **Anti-piracy organizations** These industry organizations ensure that software licensing requirements and national and international law on software usage are complied with. The three main organizations are:
  - Business Software Alliance (BSA) – This organization is active in many countries, with membership drawn from software manufacturers, varying sometimes by country. Besides other activities, the BSA provides education on software copyright issues and guidance on how to conduct self-audits. It fights software piracy in many ways, including through enforcement activities
  - Software Publishers Association (SPA) – This division of the Software & Information Industry Association (SIIA) works in the areas of education and enforcement in dealing with software management and piracy
  - Federation Against Software Theft (FAST) – This UK-based software anti-piracy organization represents both software publishers and end-users. FAST has investigators and in-house lawyers who specialize in safeguarding software publishers' intellectual property. FAST also has a consultancy branch that provides UK organizations with guidance, consultancy, training and education through its SAM services.

Making the business case

3

3 Making the business case

Successful implementation of software asset management is dependent on the establishment of a suitable culture within an organization and the commitment and support of senior business and ICT managers. Neither of these is likely unless a successful business case is produced and accepted by senior management within the organization.

> **Key message**
>
> Senior management and financial approval bodies are not primarily interested in technical arguments. To be successful, a business case must relate costs to business benefits, using sound methods of investment appraisal.

Each organization will probably have its own standards and format for business cases. The business case prepared for SAM should follow organizational standards, and should be logical, well-structured and concise. Guidance on making business cases in general can be found elsewhere. This chapter focuses on making a successful business case specifically for SAM.

3.1 DEVELOP A VISION AND STRATEGY

Before developing a business case for SAM, consideration should be given to the overall vision and strategy of the project in business terms. It is best to align these clearly with an organization's corporate or business strategy. Examples of the types of business and corporate strategies that SAM has been aligned to are:

- Improving 'time to market' for products and services
- Development of 'world-class' services and products
- Creation of more market-competitive offerings
- Driving down operating costs and increasing profitability
- Ensuring staff have quality roles and jobs
- Increasing business and employee productivity
- Ensuring continuity of business processes
- Managing business risks
- Regulatory compliance (e.g. Sarbanes-Oxley)
- Reducing the total cost of ownership of ICT systems and services, and/or increasing the return on investment (ROI).

An alternative approach is also possible, related to personal risk management for senior officers. Often senior management and directors assume that all risks associated with the use of software within an organization have been appropriately addressed by ICT management. Unfortunately, this is often not the case and the senior managers or directors, who are ultimately responsible for SAM, may be unaware of the vulnerabilities, business impacts and penalties potentially associated with poor control over software assets. Increasingly in many countries, individual directors and other officers may be held personally responsible for problems arising from areas for which they are responsible, whether or not they are exercising active control. To minimize personal exposure to risk, senior management and directors need to ensure that there are adequate systems of control in place over software assets.

The need for SAM was forcibly brought to the attention of one global organization when their offices in an Asian country were searched by the local police. The police were systematically sweeping through multi-storey buildings floor by floor and arrived at the floors occupied by this organization. Panic struck the local employees when the police refused to accept that the organization had worldwide agreements for software, and demanded to see licence documents for the software on each individual PC.

As a result of this incident, SAM became a strategic issue for this organization. However, SAM strategy should be developed proactively rather than reactively!

Vision and strategy also grow from seeing what other organizations have accomplished. To date, there has been comparatively little formal analysis and reporting of the benefits of SAM, and this is undoubtedly a factor in its limited visibility on senior management 'radar screens'. But evidence is accumulating. As part of an organization's approach to a software asset management project, feedback should be sought from other organizations that have successfully implemented SAM and the benefits they have achieved. Some examples of real-world results are given in the following box.

Note: The examples cited here are not considered extreme cases, but realistic examples of what is achievable. The savings in each case were dependent on the specific circumstances of the organizations involved, and of the licensing programs/pricing relevant for them at the time, and may not be relevant for others. Although the specific opportunities will differ for each organization, it is likely that the ones available will be significant, but they must be recognized and acted on. Most of the benefits cited here relate to savings in costs of licensing, which are often the easiest to identify. However, licensing is only a small part of TCO, and the savings in other areas may easily be much larger, although often harder to identify and measure.

- A multinational organization had a decentralized approach to the negotiation of software licences. This resulted in the overbuying of licences and poor pricing. By centralizing the process of software licence negotiation and dealing often directly with the software suppliers and publishers, more cost-effective licence agreements were obtained for the organization as a whole, saving in excess of an estimated 5 million dollars

- A major organization needed to upgrade its software. Prior to implementing SAM, its best alternative was to purchase a site agreement covering usage on all machines. After a major exercise to determine what licences it already owned, it was determined that the organization primarily needed to purchase only upgrade licences, achieving the upgrade objective at only 46% of the cost of the site agreement
- A review of software maintenance contracts at another organization revealed that maintenance was continuing to be paid on software that was no longer being used. The contracts were cancelled at a saving of over half a million euros
- A major company with a comparatively low PC:employee ratio found that it could reduce its need for client access licences (CALs) by 45%, by switching from calculating CALs on a per-person basis to a per-PC basis
- Another organization found that it could reduce existing licence usage requirements by 3% by removing software from PCs where it was not being used actively, allowing licences to be redeployed elsewhere.

3.2 INVESTIGATE THE ISSUES

3.2.1 Determine requirements

The first stage of the development of any business case is the requirements-gathering and documentation stage. This can be achieved using well-established techniques such as:

- Determining the current state of all SAM knowledge, skills, activities and processes

- Interviews with representatives from the business, including users, customers and managers
- Written questionnaire surveys of users
- Analysing software industry reports and information from consultants and specialists
- Analysing user group and industry forum and seminar reports
- Performing industry and customer surveys
- Performing risk assessments.

> **Key message**
>
> Many projects fail to deliver benefits because the business objectives are not clearly established at the outset, making it difficult to get buy-in from the business and the end-users.

The most essential part of this stage is to gather information on:

- Benefits that are priority objectives of a SAM project (see section 1.4)
- Risks that need to be addressed by the project – these include damage to the organization's reputation if there is negative publicity about under-licensing
- Cost savings
- Competitive advantage
- Workplace enrichment
- Potential stakeholders and sponsors of the project and their expectations, KPIs and CSFs and the reasons for actively supporting and driving the project to a successful conclusion
- Management attitudes towards key SAM implementation decisions that will need to be made:
  - acceptable degree of centralization of SAM functions (see section 4.1)

- acceptable degree of centralization of the SAM database (see section 4.2)
■ The potential objections to the project and measures to counter these:
  - 'It is compliance driven, but not worth having for positive benefits'
  - 'We have existed without it for years, why do it now?'
  - 'Asset management is not a priority; there are more important things to do'
  - 'The idea is too bureaucratic and not workable'
  - 'People won't accept new processes and working practices'
  - 'The SAM tool market is immature with no fully comprehensive or integrated solutions yet available'
■ The functionality required by the solution. This should be categorized as functionality that is either essential, important or 'nice to have'
■ The performance levels required by the solution: KPIs and other metrics
■ The current state of SAM activities.

3.2.2 Analyse the gap
Once the basic information has been gathered, a gap analysis should be performed between what is currently being achieved, and what is required/desired.

3.2.3 Identify and analyse alternatives
There are likely to be a significant number of implementation alternatives, depending on factors such as those described in sections 1.7 and 1.8. Each alternative should be assessed for its expected costs, benefits and timescales, as well as associated risks of failure.

The viable alternatives should be compared on an appropriate basis (which may be required by company policy), probably including TCO and ROI calculations, and a decision made as to the preferred alternative.

3.3 DOCUMENT THE BUSINESS CASE
The formal documentation of the business case should follow an organization's own requirements. Generally, it is expected to include:

■ Executive summary and recommendation as to preferred implementation alternative
■ Business requirements and benefits expected
■ Alternatives considered
■ Business impacts of each alternative: benefits, costs, risks
■ Recommended implementation plan
■ Expected realization of benefits plan (time-phased achievement of benefits).

Key message

Many business cases lack support and are rejected because they fail to relate to strategic business objectives and benefits, but concentrate on ICT and technological excellence. The key to the acceptance of a business case is to align the project visions and goals with strategic business visions and goals and to show an ROI. An example strategy for SAM is:

'To provide world-class ICT services to all customers, both internal and external, by ensuring responsive, effective, cost-efficient and legal exploitation of software assets.'

3.4 SELL THE BUSINESS CASE

Selling the business case is as important – or more so – as physically preparing it. In principle, everything that is done during the preparation of the business case is part of selling it. For example, while determining requirements it will be possible to identify people's objections and to start to counter them and convince people of the benefits that can be achieved.

A senior-level champion must be found early in the process. Without such a champion, it will be difficult to achieve the management support necessary for the real change throughout the organization required for successful implementation of SAM. Achieving budgetary approval is not enough.

The selling must also continue after the business case is approved. People who initially were not interested may become interested, but negatively. It will be better to take the time to convince them of the benefits of SAM than to ignore them or force them to go along because of senior management diktat.

The final stage to selling the business case is to prove that the project has delivered what was expected. There should be regular tracking of project progress, costs and benefits achieved during and after the project. The benefits should be addressed in a post-project review report, which should also be communicated to the ICT community and to the broader business community, to help others sell their business case.

Organization, roles and responsibilities

4

4 Organization, roles and responsibilities

A number of strategic decisions concerning organization and role assignments must be made, actively or by default, in the process of implementing and running SAM. These decisions have major time and cost implications, and even greater implications for the benefits that can be achieved.

4.1 DECISION ABOUT CENTRALIZATION

One of the most important decisions that need to be made for SAM is the degree of centralization that will be implemented, and for which functions. This is a particularly critical decision for larger organizations with multiple divisions or business units that may have significant operational autonomy.

An analogy can be made with capital expenditure. It is possible for capital expenditure decision making to be totally decentralized, but this is unusual, even in organizations that are otherwise highly decentralized. Many of the main benefits of SAM, as for capital expenditure, come from centralization. These benefits include not only cost savings, but also risk management.

As at the time of writing this guide there have not been any formal studies to quantify the impact of centralization on the benefits that SAM can bring. There are also some ways in which decentralization is superior. For example:

- Decentralization allows for greater innovation and initiative in ICT (viewed by some as 'anarchy')

- It can be easier in a geographically decentralized organization to demonstrate compliance to local authorities and regulators (although the overall cost will likely be higher than with a centralized approach)
- Some countries have requirements about the import/taxation of software that may not be easy to address within global purchasing arrangements.

However, there is considerable anecdotal evidence and logic to support the view that certain functions need to be centralized to produce the greatest possible benefits (see section 1.5).

The functions that should be centralized go beyond SAM in the narrow sense, but SAM allows them to achieve their fullest potential. These functions include in particular:

- Strategic ICT planning:
  - Use of common ICT architectures
  - Use of common products (standardization)
  - Rationalization of software and hardware deployment
- Strategic sourcing (software and hardware):
  - Selection of resellers (possibly not based in home country of headquarters)
  - Centrally negotiated pricing reflecting total purchasing power (especially important for software) and time-phased requirements (can be especially important for hardware)
- Risk management:
  - Legal compliance, including management of relationships with local authorities and compliance organizations

- Management of the impact of unexpected events on the organization, e.g. licensing audits
- Supply of software licensing expertise to the entire organization
- Coordination of reallocation of software and hardware resources between subsidiaries and business units, e.g. facilitating the redeployment of licences from units with excess, to those with growing needs.

Operational functions, however, may be handled on a more decentralized basis, including in particular:

- Procurement processing
- Deployment and installation
- Operation and maintenance of the detailed SAM database, including physical proof of licence (see section 4.2).

Key message

The overall SAM processes need to strike a balance between 'globalization' and 'localization', with responsibilities distributed appropriately between the two.

4.2 CENTRALIZATION OR DECENTRALIZATION OF SAM DATABASES

Each organization must decide how to implement its SAM database logically and physically. The decision has major time and cost implications.

In theory, the centralized functions described above would best be supported by a centralized SAM database. However, this may not be practical for a number of reasons:

- The parent company is a holding company that buys and sells subsidiaries frequently
- Different subsidiaries or business units operate largely autonomously, and a centralized SAM database would require an unacceptable level of operational centralization.

Nonetheless, it is still desirable to have a centralized SAM database to the extent consistent with operational requirements. The following approach is therefore recommended:

- The SAM database should be implemented as a physically integrated centralized database to the extent practical. In principle, this should be at the level that corresponds to operational ICT responsibility, so that there would be a consolidated SAM database for each area of autonomous ICT responsibility. Responsibility for licensing compliance should also be clearly defined at this same level. Furthermore, physical proof of licence should be controlled at this level
- SAM should be implemented in achievable modules or projects. For global organizations, getting to a truly centralized position for enterprise businesses can take years
- Information from the separate detailed SAM databases must be provided to central functions on a regular and consistent basis to allow them to perform properly
- Each SAM database may be a single physically integrated repository, or it may be a collection of freestanding but linked databases (a 'shared data environment') utilizing the capabilities of different systems and tools. Full physical integration is desirable but not easily achievable given the current state of the market for SAM and related tools.

See also Chapter 7.

4.3 RESPECTIVE ROLES OF PROCUREMENT MANAGEMENT AND ICT MANAGEMENT

Another important decision to be made concerns the respective roles of procurement management and ICT management. Responsibility for ICT procurement typically is defined in one of two ways:

■ The department responsible for procurement (called 'Procurement', or 'Purchasing', or 'Supply Chain' etc.) has principal responsibility for managing all aspects of ICT procurement, with guidance to the extent necessary from ICT management and personnel

■ The department responsible for ICT management has principal responsibility for managing all aspects of ICT procurement, with guidance to the extent necessary from procurement personnel.

Reasons for giving principal responsibility to the department responsible for procurement include:

■ It is better placed to take cold economic decisions about the cost justification of proposed expenditure, without being swayed by technology for its own sake

■ It is better prepared to deal with the legal paperwork of contracting

■ It has better negotiating skills, and can drive a harder bargain

■ It may have capacity to perform the work, compared with a possibly overworked ICT department.

Reasons for giving principal responsibility to the ICT department include:

■ ICT personnel have to live with the day-to-day consequences of procurement decisions,

and they will be more acutely focused on the operational implications of contracts and what is necessary to meet contractual obligations

■ ICT personnel may also give more attention to other non-quantifiable factors, such as the quality of licensing advice provided by resellers

■ ICT personnel have a better view on strategic ICT directions and alternatives, which is where some of the most significant savings can be identified

■ ICT personnel may have more of a 'risk management' orientation because of related ICT risk management concerns such as security and data protection.

> **Key message**
>
> On balance, assuming these expected skill profiles, it is better to give the primary responsibility for ICT procurement to the ICT department, but with a strong supporting role being played by the procurement department. If strategic procurement functions are centralized as described in section 4.1, it will be easier to ensure sufficient qualified resources are dedicated to the job from both areas.

4.4 ROLES AND RESPONSIBILITIES

If SAM processes are to prove successful within an organization, it is important that roles and responsibilities are clearly defined and agreed and that the scope of ownership of each of the processes is also defined and agreed. These roles and responsibilities should therefore be adapted to fit the individual requirements of each organization in accordance with its size, nature, structure, culture and geographical distribution.

In small organizations, one or two people will perform most of these roles.

4.4.1 Primary roles

- **Management sponsor**   It is important if SAM is to succeed within an organization that sponsorship and commitment are obtained from senior management, both within the business as a whole and the ICT department. This will ensure that the visibility of SAM is maintained and that the organizational culture is developed to enable SAM processes to succeed. It will enable sufficient budget and resources to be obtained. Therefore, management sponsorship and commitment must be maintained and not allowed to deteriorate

- **Director with legal responsibility**   SAM implementations progress to a successful conclusion more rapidly when the support and commitment of the director with the legal responsibility for software assets is clearly identified. Once identified, he or she can usually be convinced of the benefits and need for SAM throughout the organization

- **Service asset manager/configuration manager**   This is the person with overall responsibility for the service asset and configuration management process, as defined in ITIL terminology. This includes much of the scope of SAM. In an ITIL conformant organization, the individuals responsible for IT asset management and SAM might report to the configuration manager, although as defined in this guide it would mean an expansion of the role of service asset and configuration management

- **IT asset manager**   This individual should be responsible for the management of all ICT assets within an organization. He or she would have overall responsibility for establishing and maintaining the IT asset database. (This is technically part of the configuration management system [CMS] in ITIL terminology – see Chapter 9.) This database should also contain all of the information required by SAM processes. Often this asset management responsibility is distributed within the individual technical support teams (e.g. the server team manages the server assets and asset register)

- **Software asset manager**   This is the person with responsibility for the management of all software assets within an organization. This is a subset of the overall responsibility of the IT asset manager. It is essential if the responsibilities are separated that common processes and a common database are shared between the two roles. In some organizations, this role is often merged with that of the IT asset manager

- **SAM process owner/process manager**   In some organizations, responsibility for the overall effectiveness and efficiency of SAM processes rests with the SAM process owner, although they may be separated. The process manager operationally runs the process and the process owner is accountable for the process and sets high-level objectives

- **Asset analysts or configuration librarians**   These roles are responsible for maintaining up-to-date (and historical) records of IT assets, including software version control.

4.4.2 Complementary roles

- **Security manager**   This role is not strictly a part of the SAM processes but it has a crucial part to play in the operation of effective SAM processes. The security manager should help ensure that all software is maintained at the recommended security 'patch level' so that security exposures from the use of software are minimized. This role also has significant responsibilities with regard to assets, asset management and asset protection, risk assessment, management and mitigation, and security classification of assets

- **Auditors (internal and external)** These are responsible for reviewing and auditing the SAM processes for efficiency, effectiveness and compliance
- **Procurement management** This is responsible for all aspects of the procurement process within the end-user organization
- **Legal advice/council** This person is responsible for the provision of legal advice and guidance, contractual issues and legal matters
- **Change manager** This role ensures that an effective change management process is in place to control all changes within the ICT infrastructure, including all changes to software
- **Release and deployment manager** This role ensures that an only authentic licensed software is deployed to approved destinations and reviewed and audited on completion
- **SAM consultant** This person provides advice and guidance on all aspects of SAM best practice
- **Management tool analyst or automation analyst** This person is responsible for the implementation, configuring and tailoring of tools to automate processes wherever it is cost-effective
- **Service desk manager** Although this role is not strictly part of the SAM process, it is a vital one. The service desk manager has a responsibility to ensure that all contacts with the service

desk that uncover instances of unauthorized or unapproved software should be reported to the SAM exception processes as soon as possible for review and resolution.

During the implementation of SAM processes within an organization, some of the secondary roles may become primary roles for the duration of the implementation project.

Process overview

5

5 Process overview

The overall objective of all SAM processes is that of good corporate governance.

Key message

The objective of SAM is to manage, control and protect an organization's software assets, including management of the risks arising from the use of those software assets.

This guide approaches SAM principally through a description of its processes, as do ITIL, ISO/IEC 19770 and ISO/IEC 20000. An overview of the process areas for SAM is shown in Figure 5.1. These areas are similar to those for ITIL and ISO/IEC 19770 and there is also some commonality with ISO/IEC 20000. The mappings of these processes to those of ITIL, ISO/IEC 19770, ISO/IEC 20000 and COBIT (Control Objectives for Information and related Technology. Copyright 1996, 1998, 2000, The IT Governance Institute™) are described in Chapter 9.

Overall management processes		
Overall management responsibility Risk assessment Policies and procedures	Competence, awareness and training Performance metrics and continuous improvement Service continuity and availability management	
Core asset management processes		
Asset identification Asset control Status accounting	Database management Financial management	
Logistics processes Requirements definition Design Evaluation Procurement Build Deployment Operation Optimization Retirement	**Verification and compliance processes** Verification and audit Licensing compliance Security compliance Other compliance	**Relationship processes** Contract management Supplier management Internal business relationship management Outsourcing management

Figure 5.1 SAM process areas

This chapter gives:

- An overview of the objectives and constituent activities of each of the process areas of SAM
- Detailed comments where appropriate about each of the process areas.

The comments given are limited to clarifying the scope of SAM processes, as there is already ample discussion in several ITIL publications and other professional materials about most other relevant generic areas, e.g. IT service continuity and availability management. More detail is given in this guide only where it is important for a proper understanding of SAM. The logistics processes in particular require the most detailed comments, in particular the procurement process.

5.1 OVERALL MANAGEMENT PROCESSES

Objective

To establish and maintain the management infrastructure within which the other SAM processes are implemented.

5.1.1 Overall management responsibility

Senior management has overall responsibility for all aspects of corporate governance. Increasingly, these responsibilities are being codified in different corporate governance standards, such as Turnbull in the UK and Sarbanes-Oxley in the USA, although these guidelines are also used in many other countries. The overall responsibility for SAM should be explicitly linked into these standards to the extent possible.

As part of this issue, it is critical to ensure that responsibility for SAM is clearly defined within the remit of specific positions. While this may be simple in principle, in practice it is often not done, with the result that nobody takes responsibility. For example, a board of directors may consider its group head of ICT to have overall responsibility for SAM, including compliance issues. However, in practice this individual may not have the remit or authority to ensure appropriate systems for SAM throughout the organization. This is typically a problem in organizations with decentralized management structures but a central ICT unit providing some, but not all, ICT services.

5.1.2 Risk assessment

Management is responsible for making and regularly updating assessments of risks to which the organization is exposed. Ultimately, these assessments are the drivers for most of the other control actions taken by the organization, including SAM. The major risk areas for SAM are listed in section 1.5.

5.1.3 Policies and procedures

Management is responsible for ensuring that appropriate policies and procedures are put in place to achieve appropriate SAM throughout the organization. Most important is a clear central statement of SAM policy, which is effectively communicated throughout the organization with mechanisms to ensure periodic employee acknowledgement. An example of such a policy statement is included in Appendix F. The mechanisms used to promulgate such policies will typically be used to promulgate other critical corporate policies, such as on information confidentiality and security measures.

5.1.4 Competence, awareness and training

Management needs to ensure that relevant personnel have appropriate levels of competence. For example, licensing is a complex area and it requires a reasonable level of competence to manage correctly. Normally it is desirable to have this competence in-house. It may be possible to rely on a commercial partner (e.g. a reseller) to provide much assistance in this area, but ultimately the responsibility for compliance is with the organization itself, and not with the reseller. This knowledge of licensing issues must be kept up to date as the terms and conditions of software usage frequently change.

All employees should also typically have a level of general awareness of SAM and licensing requirements. Some volume-licensing agreements make such awareness efforts a contractual requirement. This awareness can be achieved via the same mechanisms that are used to communicate policies to employees.

5.1.5 Performance metrics and continuous improvement

The overall management processes have responsibility for performance management of the SAM processes, including:

- Definition of measurements, metrics and KPIs
- Performance monitoring, reporting and reviewing
- Continuous process improvement (Plan–Do–Check–Act).

5.1.6 IT service continuity management and availability management

The overall management processes include responsibility for IT service continuity management and availability management related to SAM. This responsibility includes ensuring that:

- The SAM database is backed up and protected by appropriate availability and contingency measures
- There is reasonable security for all assets and all proofs of licence, with adequate backup records in case of events such as fire
- The organization's contingency provisions are themselves subject to proper SAM, e.g. that hot backup systems are properly licensed.

Key message

Licensing assets, including proof of licence, need to be properly stored and protected. Loss of these assets may require replacement through repurchase. In some cases, these licences may no longer be available for sale. If they are available, there might be new terms and conditions that could even affect the original installation. Proper care of licensing assets avoids all of these issues.

5.2 CORE ASSET MANAGEMENT PROCESSES

Objective

To identify and to maintain information about software assets throughout their lifecycle, and to manage physical assets related to software.

Traditionally, asset management has been seen as the maintenance of an asset register and a set of processes for managing the financial aspects of purchasing, depreciation and retirement of an organization's assets. However, it is actually much broader than this.

5.2.1 Asset identification

Each organization needs to define the asset items it needs to control as part of its SAM system, and the attributes it needs for each asset. A distinction should be made between the items to be controlled, and the inventory system for those items. The asset items that usually need to be controlled are:

- A secure software library of master copies and media and the definitive media library (DML), together with controlled distributed copies
- Licences purchased
- Contractual documentation (agreements, licence terms and conditions etc.)
- Other proof of licence (licence confirmations etc.)
- Installed software
- Standard configuration definitions/instances (with base-lining as planned, as released and as installed with fixes/updates)
- Financial data (for management and financial accounting and for tax purposes)
- Management of related vendor information and related maintenance and support information.

See Appendix C for suggestions about the contents of a SAM database. It is essential that the appropriate hardware assets are also recorded and managed as many licence costs are based on the hardware servers etc. on which they run.

5.2.2 Asset control

Asset control ensures that assets are controlled and authorized through their lifecycle. It is closely linked to some of the logistics processes.

5.2.3 Status accounting

Status accounting provides an audit trail of changes in the status of assets through the stages of the lifecycle.

5.2.4 Database management

Database management as defined in this guide is focused on the purely technical and housekeeping aspects of the SAM database. It consists of:

- Database design and optimization
- All relevant housekeeping activities on the SAM database.

5.2.5 Financial management

Financial management is one of the core processes within SAM. For any organization, relevant cost information should be captured, not just for software assets themselves, but also for related processes, to help justify SAM finances and budgets and overall process improvements. SAM financial management includes:

- Ensuring the preparation of reliable financial information for all software assets, including during their procurement, operation (e.g. regular depreciation) and subsequent retirement and disposal
- Collecting cost/benefit information related to the use of software assets, to allow the calculation of TCO and ROI
- Ensuring that there is appropriate financial approval for all new software procurement
- Proper consideration of accounting and tax treatments.

Relevant expertise should be used to ensure that accounting and tax treatments for software assets are appropriate and tax efficient. Depending on the country involved and other factors such as tax position and industry, significant tax savings may be possible through a combination of good record-keeping and proper application of the relevant tax regulations.

5.3 LOGISTICS PROCESSES

> **Objective**
>
> To control all activities affecting the progress of software through its lifecycle.

The logistics processes of SAM map to the stages of the application lifecycle, which is an expansion of the service lifecycle (Figure 5.2).

This application lifecycle has been extended for this guide (Figure 5.3) to encompass the additional stages required for externally sourced software. The SAM logistics processes are the same as the processes in this modified application lifecycle.

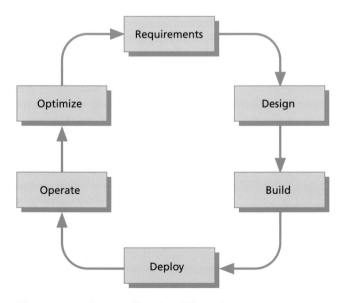

Figure 5.2 The application lifecycle

The logistics processes may need to be applied at any level of activity from highly extensive to the relatively minor:

- A major ICT project based on a new architecture and infrastructure will dictate extensive attention to all of the lifecycle steps
- An end-user online request for the automated installation of a new application (from a list of pre-approved alternatives) using pull technology will also be covered by the application lifecycle, within the context of pre-established blanket approvals.

SAM logistical processes enable the right software to be delivered to the right locations with the right quality and within the right timescale. The trigger for the commencement of logistics activity should be the initiation of a change within the change management process, as defined in ITIL terminology. This trigger event could be: a major corporate reassessment of ICT strategy; a software manufacturer announcement of product obsolescence; an individual ICT project proposal; or a request by an individual user for the installation of a new application. However major or minor, the process requirements as defined in this section should apply to all such situations, with a corresponding degree of complexity or simplicity in the application of these requirements.

5.3.1 Requirements definition

The initial stage of any software product involves the requirements-gathering and definition stage. This is the most important stage of the lifecycle and is where the business needs are identified and documented with regard to any new requirements. Information and data obtained from the SAM processes and tools are often essential to these requirements-gathering activities.

These requirements should include all aspects of the software, including the functional requirements, the non-functional requirements and the usability requirements. It should also incorporate all of the intended service targets for the 'operate' stage of the lifecycle within a service level requirement (SLR) document.

The functional requirements are those specifically required to support a business process. Non-functional requirements address the operational and management needs. The principal involvement of SAM is an important non-functional requirement that ensures all of the needs of SAM within the subsequent stages of the software

lifecycle are included within the overall set of requirements.

Once the requirements have been agreed and documented, the business case, feasibility study and cost–benefit analysis should be completed. The project should only progress to subsequent stages of the lifecycle if the results of these analyses indicate appropriate business benefits will be realized.

Another issue that may need to be considered within a requirements exercise is upgrading software. The upgrade of software also needs to consider:

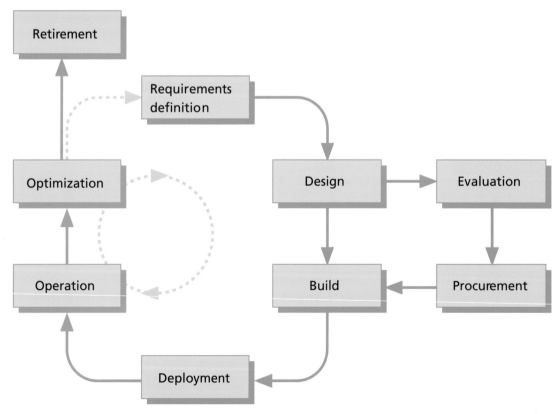

Figure 5.3 The modified application lifecycle (including externally sourced software)

- Do we need a new release, version or patch level of the software (e.g. increased required functionality)?
- What are the business benefits deriving from its usage (e.g. increased business productivity or improved product performance)?
- What are the risks associated with continuing with the existing release, version or patch level (e.g. manufacturer has withdrawn support of the existing product)?

5.3.2 Design

Design for in-house developed software includes the design of the application itself together with the design of the environment or operational model within which the application has to run. For externally sourced software, often 'blueprint' operational models are built and tested to ensure conformance to functional requirements, and consistency and integration with other systems within the organization.

Consideration should be given to the applications architecture, systems architecture and the management architecture within the overall design, to ensure that any development or 'blueprint' operational models are consistent with the overall organizational strategies and policies.

5.3.3 Evaluation

The evaluation stage is primarily for externally sourced software although some aspects may be appropriate where in-house applications are being designed and developed. Formal terms of reference (ToR) and statement of requirements (SoR) documents may be produced and circulated to prospective suppliers. Evaluation criteria and processes are also documented for the assessment of alternative proposals and may also be circulated

to prospective suppliers. The proposal that 'best fits' the evaluation criteria should be selected for implementation.

This stage may also include aspects of design and design evaluation, although principally the design will be part of overall information systems (IS) and ICT strategies. All of the ongoing operational needs of SAM should be considered and evaluated at this point and must be met by the selected solution.

This stage will include the selection of the most cost-effective software licensing agreements.

5.3.4 Procurement

This stage of the lifecycle is primarily for externally sourced software and is entered once the evaluation process has been completed and the most appropriate solution has been selected. It may also be necessary to complete some of the activities within this stage for in-house developed software if hardware or additional software is required, e.g. development software or runtime licences for production software.

Even though SAM is actively involved in the previous logistics stages, with procurement the need for good SAM becomes especially critical. If appropriate procurement processes are not followed correctly and consistently, problems will be created that will be costly and difficult to detect and subsequently correct.

The sub-processes of SAM procurement are illustrated in Figure 5.4. The flow through the sub-processes is dependent on whether distribution copies and sufficient licences are already available for use within the organization, and on contractual requirements for when licences must be ordered (e.g. before installing, monthly after installing or yearly after installing). More detailed comments are also given about some of the sub-processes.

5.3.4.1 Process internal order

During the processing of an internal order, a check should be made as to whether there are already any available licences free to be used. These may be available, for example, because there was a bulk purchase which has not all been used up or licences are free because of retirement or rationalization of deployment elsewhere. A centralized view of licence availability gives the best cost-saving opportunity, especially for large organizations with many units operating largely autonomously. (There also need to be corresponding procedures to formally transfer the licences if management is handled on a decentralized basis.)

5.3.4.2 Initiate external order

A consistent finding in many organizations is that there is poor coordination of purchasing arrangements, with the result that purchases are often made that do not take advantage of the best available alternatives. For example, a business unit may purchase a product locally at retail prices rather than through a centralized and more cost-effective contract. The process for initiating the external order should ensure that the most appropriate source is chosen for fulfilling the order.

5.3.4.3 Process proof of licence

There are two main cases to consider for processing proof of licence, and each has a major issue associated with it:

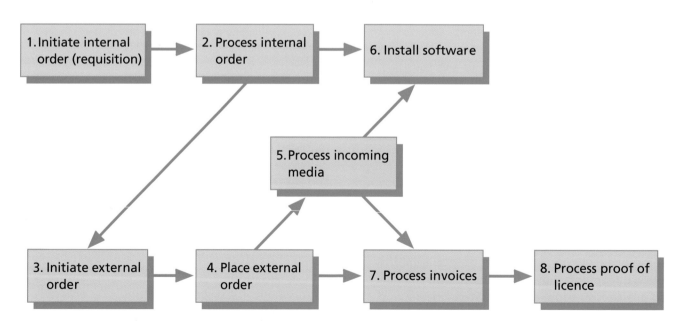

Figure 5.4 The SAM procurement process

■ **Non-volume and OEM proof of licence** These licences do not name the licensee. The main concern is to ensure the product's authenticity, i.e. that it is not counterfeit

■ **Volume proof of licence** These name the licensee. The main concern is to ensure that the required documentation from the software manufacturer in the customer's name is actually received.

Each of these is dealt with briefly below:

■ **Ensuring product authenticity** There is a serious risk of organizations purchasing counterfeit software through non-volume-licensing channels. In part this is because of the attractiveness of this market to counterfeiters, and in part, because of the limited attention often paid to product authenticity by end-user organizations, and sometimes even by resellers and distributors. The organization should make reasonable checks for the authenticity of the software it is purchasing, especially when risk factors for counterfeiting are elevated. See section A.4 for a discussion of counterfeiting, and what an organization should do about it

> **Warning**
>
> The biggest 'red flag' for counterfeit software is low price.
>
> If one reseller charges significantly less than another reseller for the same quantity of the same product, beware of counterfeits. Explanations of 'grey imports' or 'clearance stock' are likely to be deceptions.
>
> Ensure that you get a breakdown of hardware and software costs for any package deals offered.

■ **Ensuring receipt of volume proof of licence** Another important issue in the procurement process is checking for the receipt of the volume proof of licence. This is complicated by the fact that many volume-licensing situations involve a tri-partite relationship, with the order going to a reseller, but with the licence confirmation coming back from the software manufacturer. It is possible to insist on receiving the licence confirmation before payment, similar to situations involving physical delivery of goods. However, this will often be problematical because of the impact it will have on reseller cashflow. As a result, an alternative procedure can be used, as indicated in Figure 5.5.

The licence confirmation may be physical or electronic. Note that if the software manufacturer licence confirmation is not received directly from the software manufacturer, it should also be checked for authenticity. There have been cases of counterfeit volume-licensing confirmations.

5.3.5 Build

The build stage is extensively used with in-house developed software, and it is also relevant for creating new builds of externally sourced software. For in-house developed software, it encompasses the development, coding, integration, building and testing of all of the components within the new release. This should involve the use of separate development, build and test environments. All of these environments should mirror the proposed live environments as closely as possible. Once these build and test activities have been completed, the approved release can be deployed throughout the organization.

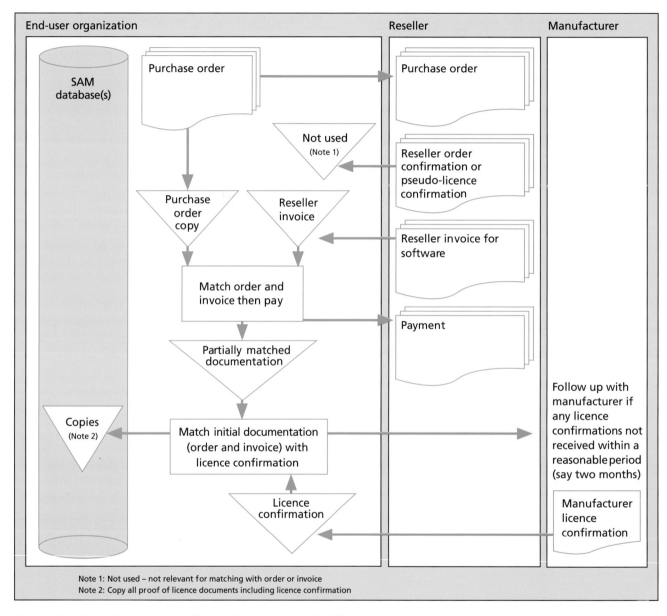

Figure 5.5 Checking receipt of manufacturer proof of licence

For externally sourced software, this stage consists of integration, building and extensive testing. Once complete the approved release can be deployed throughout the organization.

This process will ensure that only correct versions of software that are 'fit for purpose' will be released to the organization, minimizing the disruption often caused by problems with new releases. Often pilot tests are completed prior to full deployment to minimize the risk and disruption to the business and accomplish this release in a controlled manner. In some organizations, a staging environment is used to rigorously test new releases before distribution to the live environment. The ongoing requirements of the SAM processes should also be built and tested within each of these environments, e.g. the ability of discovery tools to identify properly the new software or versions.

SAM should help ensure that the release consists only of those components that are approved for release and that all components are authentic, licensed, supported and legal. SAM should also ensure that all of the proposed destination environments have the necessary contracts and licences.

5.3.6 Deployment

During the deployment stage, all components of a release are deployed to their agreed and approved destination environments. SAM is responsible for monitoring the deployment process so that software is only deployed to the environment for which licences and contracts have been obtained. It is essential that during this process the details contained within the SAM database are updated to reflect the progress of the deployment project in a timely fashion. This is the stage where the most non-compliances can be introduced with regard to the use of unlicensed software within an organization.

The deployment mechanisms used may vary significantly depending on the extensiveness of the deployment required. Physical deployment may be required, especially if new hardware is also involved. Push technologies are useful for mass deployments to machines determined by ICT, including for security patches and anti-virus updates. Pull technologies are especially useful for deployment to individuals requesting specific applications where approval can be automated or where there is pre-approval. These are areas of considerable focus by ICT departments independent of any formal focus on SAM. However, the deployment process needs to be integrated into SAM to ensure that all deployments are properly authorized, including having licences, and that the SAM database is properly updated as a result.

There is one important licensing 'exception condition' that deployment functionality must be able to handle. This is deployment of software to machines that are already properly licensed, e.g. where software must be reinstalled because of hardware failure or major software problems, but there is no need to purchase additional licences. The exposure here is that this procedural loophole could be abused to install additional unauthorized software. Procedures should ensure that reinstallations are supported by checking for proper prior authorizations just as for new installations.

Another issue that must be addressed during deployment is the handling of licensing terms and conditions that frequently must be accepted during the installation of software, both commercial and non-commercial. Such terms may even authorize the installation of 'spy-ware' and other unintended functionality. If software has been properly tested before deployment, this issue will already have been addressed. The main concern lies with employees who may be able to install software independently.

5.3.7 Operation

This stage of the lifecycle is responsible for monitoring exceptions in ongoing operations relevant to SAM. There are two major aspects to this activity:

- Ensuring that the ICT services are operated, supported and managed according to the service targets agreed within the original SLRs, which should now evolve into SLAs for the operational services. Example targets would be deployment time for security patches, and workstation overheads for running metering tools
- Identifying individual exceptions to SAM policies, e.g. identifying instances of unauthorized software installed on workstations immediately or soon after installation.

There is overlap between these requirements, and the requirements of the two other areas listed below, with the differentiator being whether exceptions are identified on an immediate basis or on a periodic basis. These areas are:

- Compliance processes – see section 5.4
- Performance metrics and continuous improvement – see section 5.1.5.

5.3.8 Optimization

Optimization is a process that overlaps with general management processes, with the objective being to ensure continuous improvement. This focus on improvement can operate in several areas:

- **Software deployment optimization** Active software usage (as opposed to just installation or availability) should be reviewed periodically to determine whether deployment corresponds to end-user needs. It may also be appropriate to conduct end-user surveys of software that is considered necessary. A common finding is that there may be significant levels of software deployed that are not being actively used. Depending on licensing terms and conditions, it may be possible to redeploy these unnecessary licences to other users or locations where they are needed. While the savings may be limited initially, as purchased licences generally cannot be returned, future savings may be achieved by avoiding additional purchases for other users
- **Performance targets** Service performance achievements, targets, usage and fit-for-purpose levels should be continuously monitored and wherever they are threatened or breached, action should be initiated to prevent such occurrences in the future. This will necessitate a continuous improvement process within the operational and optimization stages of the lifecycle as indicated in Figure 5.3. Some of the actions may also drive more major processes, e.g. the development of new systems capabilities to achieve required improvements
- **Overall efficiency and effectiveness** It should also be an integral aspect of this part of the software lifecycle to continually assess the SAM processes for efficiency and effectiveness and to feed back suggested improvements whenever possible. This should include reviews for optimization and supportability with partners and suppliers (e.g. when a supplier may stop

supporting a version for reason of age, or when licence conditions are changed or should be changed).

5.3.9 Retirement

The final stage of the lifecycle is the retirement phase. (This is sometimes referred to as the 'write-off' phase, but write-offs may happen before retirement for tax efficiency purposes or because of long asset life. Therefore, retirement is not the same as write-off, even though they may often happen together.) Retirement occurs when services and systems cease to be functional or be available for any reason, or are no longer cost-effective to use. Once it is decided to retire a software asset, it needs to be dealt with appropriately. Often software remains within the operational environment, but is not subject to patches, upgrades, support etc. This can cause licensing and communications issues and needs to be managed with the software progressed into retirement. Many potential issues need to be considered in relation to software retirement:

- **Hardware retirement** Software retirement is often associated with the retirement of hardware, and needs to be dealt with appropriately:
  - OEM software: Normally, OEM software that was supplied with hardware can only be used with that hardware, so it cannot be 'recycled'. However, the relevant proof of OEM licences will normally make the equipment more valuable on the secondary market, so these original materials can be disposed of together with the hardware (if they have been properly stored and are accessible)
  - non-OEM software: Often, the licences for non-OEM software (including upgrades previously applied to OEM software) are transferable to other hardware. In these cases, the installed version cannot be left on the hardware when it is disposed. In any case, it is normally desirable to wipe hard disks to remove confidential data, which will also have the effect of removing the software. If the licences being moved are upgrades that were originally applied to OEM licences, it will be necessary to have another properly qualified underlying licence for any machine to which it is transferred

- **Retirement of deployment, but not of licences** Sometimes a version of software will be retired, or even a complete product, so there will be no more installations of the specific software. However, the licences themselves will not be retired, but rather provide a basis for upgrade licences. In these cases, the installed versions of the software will need to be uninstalled, but the licences will need to be retained and linked to the new licences which will be based on them

- **Options for recycling** Where software and licences are both being retired, it may be possible to consider recycling alternatives, depending on detailed licensing terms and conditions:
  - transfer/sale to related organizations: Licensing terms and conditions, including those under volume-licensing contracts, often allow for transfer of licences to related companies, perhaps with specific procedural and notification requirements
  - transfer/sale to unrelated organizations: Non-volume-licensing terms and conditions

(including retail and OEM) often allow for transfer of licences to anyone, subject to full transfer of all relevant materials. Volume-licensing contracts may also allow this, but more often require the formal consent of the software manufacturer. There is no guarantee of success, but if the amounts involved are significant, and there is a realistic market, then it is probably worth checking with the manufacturer

- ■ **Archiving** It is good practice to archive a copy of all retired software. It might be necessary at some future date to restore retired software to access historical data, for example, to meet statutory requirements for access to information supporting financial statements or tax returns. There might be licensing implications for such archiving, and these should be investigated. Contractual conditions could be negotiated initially to ensure that such future needs are covered.

5.4 VERIFICATION AND COMPLIANCE PROCESSES

Objective

To detect, escalate and manage all exceptions to SAM policies, processes, procedures and licence use rights.

Figure 5.6 illustrates how the compliance processes relate to the SAM database and to real-world instances.

Compliance processes must include sub-processes for identifying and resolving SAM exception conditions and non-compliances.

No matter how comprehensive and extensive the SAM processes are there will always be some areas of non-compliance. Any truly effective SAM processes will have automated methods for trapping these non-compliances and escalating them to the appropriate resources for immediate attention. The SAM processes should not only be capable of trapping and escalating non-compliances but should also instigate remedial action to processes and procedures wherever possible to prevent recurrences.

5.4.1 Verification and audit

The objective of the verification and audit process is to ensure that the SAM records accurately reflect what is actually held, and that appropriate corrective actions are undertaken when discrepancies are identified. There are two main issues to address here:

- ■ Whether asset counts and related information are accurate
- ■ Whether the underlying assets – especially licences – are genuine, i.e. not counterfeit.

5.4.1.1 Accurate records

The process used for verifying the integrity of records of software is one of the most fully developed in the market. In particular, there are a large number of software 'discovery' tools that help to identify software in use. Care needs to be taken when selecting and implementing these tools, because the level and scope of identification, recognition and recording varies considerably between the discovery tools available. Further information about these tools is given in Chapter 7.

In spite of the comparatively advanced state of this type of tool, there are still major restrictions that need to be noted:

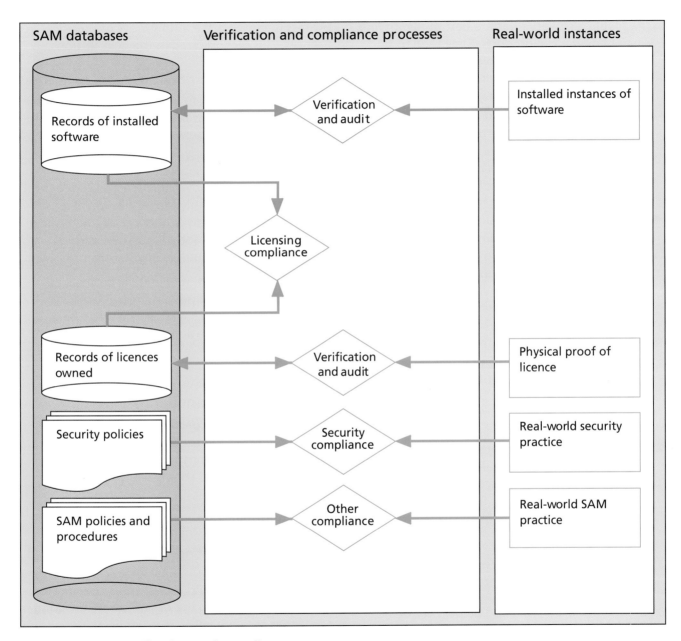

Figure 5.6 SAM verification and compliance processes

■ Available discovery tools are best at identifying major commercial products. They tend to be weak at identifying the following types of products, which generally require extensive work to identify adequately:
- in-house developed products, including identification of versions and patches applied
- software that end-users are particularly liable to install without proper authorization, such as file-swapping software and instant messaging programs

■ Most discovery tools will provide a list of what has been found, which will not necessarily be all software. This has to be subsequently reconciled with recorded assets. Often the task can become complicated when multiple versions of an application are in use due to upgrades and releases

■ Available discovery tools are often limited in the platforms on which they can be used. This is an issue not just for different types of workstation machine, but also for personal digital assistants (PDAs), SmartPhones and other mobile devices

■ Discovery tools are strongest in networked environments. There will always be complications of using discovery tools for non-networked machines, e.g. for free-standing dedicated uses, or for mobile machines that are connected rarely.

Verifying the integrity of records of licences held is a manually intensive activity. The main work should be performed when the records are initially created, but there should also be periodic or continuous processes to confirm the continuing accuracy and completeness of records held. One of the main issues to be addressed as part of this process is verifying the authenticity of proof of licences. This is considered in the next section.

5.4.1.2 Verification of authenticity of licences

There is a small but very real risk of organizations purchasing counterfeit licences, especially if they purchase through 'grey' import channels. These problems occur not only for small businesses buying from bargain sources, but also for major organizations, both governmental and commercial. The risks to the company are, at the very least, those of not having any licences at all. Depending on the circumstances, local legislation and enforcement, they could be much worse.

Licence authenticity should initially be checked as part of the original procurement process, as described in section 5.3.4. There may also be a periodic review of the authenticity of existing licences following the same principles as described in that section.

5.4.2 Licensing compliance

Licensing compliance processes are responsible for ensuring that the use of all software within an organization remains within all legal and contractual terms and conditions. Licensing compliance consists of:

■ Identification, alerting, capture and resolution of all exception conditions and non-conformances relating to the use of unlicensed software. These should include:
- identification and review of all changes in software within the organization, ensuring that they are within current licensing agreements
- interception of any SAM abnormalities recorded by the service desk, incident management, security management, release

and deployment management or any other process

- interception and detection of any unapproved software purchases
- escalation or feedback mechanisms for the instigation of reactive and remedial actions, relating to software licensing

- Correction and prevention of licensing shortfalls
- Identification and highlighting of software overuse and redundancy situations.

5.4.3 Security compliance

A compliance programme should address compliance with security policies and standards and should ensure that:

- Software policies are consistent with security policies and plans
- All security patches are being applied promptly to all relevant machines.

5.4.4 Other compliance

A compliance programme should address compliance with all other significant policies and procedures, including the overall SAM policies and procedures. It should ensure:

- SAM polices are consistent with all other corporate policies and strategies
- The impact of non-compliance (to the organization and to the individual, e.g. loss of job) is well communicated to all employees
- Implementation of all cost-justifiable preventive mechanisms, such as for preventing unauthorized software downloads from the internet and inhibiting attachment of certain file types to emails.

5.5   RELATIONSHIP MANAGEMENT PROCESSES

Objective

To manage all relationships within the business, and with partners and suppliers, to agreed contractual, legal and documented service terms and targets.

Both internal and external relationships need to be managed. External relationships that need to be managed include those with software manufacturers and their resellers, and also any outsourcers who are providing related services internally. Internal relationships that need to be managed include those with both management and end-users.

External partners (software manufacturers, resellers, outsourcers etc.) may be sources of significant information. For example, they may be able to provide records of licences purchased as a check on, or possibly in place of, internal records that may be incomplete. The main roles of this process are:

- Overall coordination, negotiation and management of all contracts and licence costs and agreements with all software suppliers and resellers
- Overall coordination and management of all relationships with the customers and the business.

5.5.1 Contract management

Contract management is a specialized aspect of external partner management that deserves separate discussion. Contract management includes:

■ Review, negotiation and management of all software contracts including the structuring of software contracts
■ Monitoring of supplier performance to ensure suppliers meet or exceed their contracted service levels.

Proper contract structuring is an important aspect of SAM. Where possible, contracts should be structured to reflect the lines of responsibility for SAM. For example, in a decentralized organization, it will typically facilitate licence management if each separate unit managing its own software has its own sub-agreement for reporting purposes. The alternative (centralized reporting) can make it difficult to reconcile orders to licence confirmations, to identify licences at the time of demergers and, in general, to manage licences at the level where SAM responsibility lies.

Software 'maintenance' or 'insurance' contracts need to be monitored against software releases, to ensure all available upgrade rights are identified, even if not immediately utilized.

5.5.2 Supplier management

Supplier management includes the management of relationships with all software suppliers, resellers, partners and software manufacturers, including regular review meetings and the agreement of contract or SLA performance measurements, metrics and KPIs. This is principally to ensure that contract expectations are clearly set out and understood, all software is purchased from reputable sources and that the suppliers, resellers, partners and software manufacturers are reputable, have a long-term future and are providing value for money. The management of software suppliers, resellers and partners should be consistent with the overall supplier management processes and the supplier and contracts database (SCD) as detailed within the supplier management section of *Service Design* (TSO, 2007).

5.5.3 Internal business relationship management

Internal business relationship management (BRM) includes the management of the relationship with internal business managers on all aspects related to software and its use within the organization. This may be done directly with the business managers or may be through a centralized point of contact within the ICT organization such as the service level manager, an account manager or a business relationship manager.

Internal BRM also includes the provision of adequate training and education on the relevant SAM aspects for customers and users of software, ensuring recognition of the software policy and its use.

5.5.4 Outsourcing

Outsourcing is a special case of managing an external supplier who performs a role, function or process typically kept in-house. The range of such situations includes:

■ **Basic activities** – roll-outs, or ongoing technical support, provided by operational suppliers
■ **Intermediate activities** – procurement etc., provided by tactical suppliers

- **Extensive activities** – turn-key, outsourcing agreements, managed services etc., e.g. for asset management, provided by strategic suppliers.

More detail on operational, tactical and strategic suppliers and the categorization of suppliers can be found in section 4.7 on supplier management in *Service Design* (TSO, 2007). Most of the comments already made about both internal and external relationships apply. Additional issues that need to be considered include:

- Conflicts of interest regarding sharing of asset information, especially with multiple outsourcers
- Possible negative effects of compensation criteria (e.g. an outsourcer may be paid based on the number of hardware devices managed, with the result that hardware savings will probably not be in the outsourcer's best interest)
- Need to clarify who has ownership of licences
- Termination implications, e.g. transfer of licence ownership.

There is also a potential issue when an outsourcer is responsible for installing software, whether as part of a major roll-out, or for one-off installations of software by technical support personnel. There is a significant risk that the responsibility for licences will not be clearly defined, with the result that each side thinks the other is responsible for obtaining software licences. The risk is ultimately with the end-user organization, so it should be clearly stated contractually if the outsourcer is to provide the licences and what the terms of ownership and maintenance will be. There should be appropriate follow-up to ensure that the relevant proof of licence is obtained.

5.6 SPECIAL SITUATIONS

Several special situations may create risk that needs to be managed.

5.6.1 Mergers/demergers and reorganizations

Software asset management, and licensing in particular, is often overlooked as part of mergers and demergers. Proper 'due diligence' at these times should ensure that SAM is understood, including licence ownership and novation. If this is not done, the acquiring company may be acquiring an unexpected financial and legal exposure due to inadequate licensing. Or a demerged company may subsequently find itself without adequate software licences.

There may be special procedural or documentation requirements for such situations, which must be determined by reference to contractual documentation or software manufacturers. There may also be some limitations as to the transferability of some licences, e.g. the non-divisibility of some volume licences. There are also times when divesting or merger firms require special 'rights to use' agreements with software manufacturers/suppliers.

Similar considerations may apply to internal reorganizations, especially if they affect the organization, geographical location or responsibility for ICT assets. As discussed in section 4.2, it is recommended that licensing documentation is held at the same place as the operational responsibility for licensing compliance.

5.6.2 Downsizing

Downsizing will usually result in inventories of unused licences, which may be redeployed elsewhere in the organization or potentially sold to third parties. It is recommended that these issues should be discussed with the software manufacturers first if the intention is to sell the licences to third parties.

One difficult issue to address is how to deal with downsizing of an organization that was not originally fully licensed. Legally, the obligation to purchase licences was incurred when software was initially used, and did not disappear when usage ceased.

5.6.3 Novation (customer/reseller/ manufacturer legal changes)

The requirement for novation may arise when an organization reforms itself and wishes to transfer all of its existing contracts and assets to the new organization. This situation occurs, for example, within central and local government organizations, when departments, agencies and complete organizations are restructured. It is necessary in these situations that all suppliers and resellers are contacted to inform them that all of the assets and contracts have novated across to the new organization.

Novation is not an automatic right, and it may be desirable to consider this right during original contract negotiations. The supplier (and sometimes the customer) may use the occasion of novation to insist on renegotiating the contract, including changes to the terms and conditions, volume discount, the actual price and the rights that the purchaser has (i.e. they may not be able to use it in the same way or the same people may not be able to use it as before).

Implementation overview

6

6 Implementation overview

The most difficult aspect of any process is its initial implementation. This has to be achieved while maintaining normal 'business as usual' processes and workloads. The implementation of SAM processes is no different, and can be broken down into four distinct stages as shown in Figure 6.1.

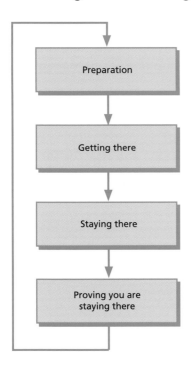

Figure 6.1 SAM implementation

One person should be appointed to own all of these stages and to run the initial project of establishing efficient SAM processes. Ideally, this same person should also own and be accountable for all of the ongoing and improvement aspects of the SAM processes. Where possible, processes already in existence within the organization should be used or adapted to fit the required SAM solution. It should be emphasized that a programme of evaluation and assessment should be undertaken by the organization to identify effective processes and build on them as appropriate.

6.1 PREPARATION

Adequate preparation is always a critical success factor for any implementation. As a minimum, this stage should consist of the following elements:

■ Reviewing the current situation with regard to the existing level of the management of software assets

■ Scoping and sizing the task, developing an outline project plan of the stages, timescales, activities, costs and risks associated with the implementation of SAM, using a structured project management methodology. This would involve:

● conducting sample surveys to determine the size and nature of the challenge for implementing SAM. This should include all aspects of the ICT infrastructure including server systems, network systems, PCs, PDAs etc.

● ultimately, this will require as a minimum the development and maintenance of a complete hardware and software inventory database. This is the basis of any set of SAM processes

■ Defining a vision and a desired state for the implementation of SAM within the organization, including objectives, deliverables, measurements, metrics, KPIs and CSFs. All of these should be defined for the overall SAM process and for each of the constituent processes

- Agreeing and appointing ownership and responsibility for the SAM processes and their implementation. There may be different people responsible for the ownership of different SAM processes during the implementation project and the subsequent ongoing operation of the processes
- Identifying and assessing software risks and creating a risk register
- Producing a business case justifying the approach to SAM within the organization (see Chapter 3)
- Obtaining sign-off, commitment and sponsorship for the project from both the business and IT, including the commitment of the necessary budget and resources for the successful implementation of the project
- Preventing a worsening situation, by identifying 'stop-gap' processes to prevent greater use of uncontrolled software within the organization
- Highlighting any problems and raising the profile of continued non-conformance
- Raising the awareness of the situation within both the business and IT, producing communication, education and training plans for all areas of the organization
- Identifying 'quick wins' to help obtain buy-in to the project
- Producing and agreeing an implementation project plan together with agreed budgets, resources and responsibilities, including the identification of associated issues and risks,

together with all cost-effective mitigation actions
- Designing the overall SAM process and scoping all of the constituent processes, as detailed in Chapter 5
- Reviewing the SAM tools and database(s) for the comprehensiveness of their content and solution in underpinning the roles and processes.

How do you know when you are prepared? Consider the following questions:

- Has sponsorship for the SAM project been committed to at a senior management or board level?
- Has the profile of SAM been raised within the organization and is the SAM culture developing?
- Have the vision and strategy for SAM been documented and agreed?
- Has the business case been accepted and approved?
- Have the budget and resources been committed to and are they available?
- Has a detailed plan been produced and accepted?

6.2 GETTING THERE

The second stage consists of implementing the agreed project plan, ensuring that the project meets all of its proposed targets:

- Managing and implementing the agreed plan
- Developing an overall software policy encompassing all aspects of software and its use within the organization (see Appendix F)

- Accepting and agreeing to the overall policy by senior management within the business and ICT and the commitment and support to its implementation in all areas of the organization
- Distributing, publicizing, communicating, implementing and enforcing the software policy throughout the organization. It is essential that the policy is universally accepted and implemented in all areas of the organization as a company standard
- Developing a corporate culture within the organization in which all personnel understand the difference between the use of approved and unapproved software
- Reviewing the risk register and the implementation of appropriate risk mitigation actions using cost-justifiable countermeasures
- Designing, developing and implementing an accurate and comprehensive set of SAM databases
- Creating a 'ring-fenced' store of the master media of all approved, operational software in use within the organization. The storage details of all media should be recorded within the SAM database, including details of the original supplier of the software and format of the data. A detailed record of any software media taken from the store of master media should be kept, signing in and out the media with reasons for its use and a signature by the individual taking it. The master software media should be kept under lock and key at all times, possibly in a safe to minimize associated risks
- Creating a repository for the protection and retention of all software contracts, authenticity certificates and licence agreements. The storage details of all documents should be recorded within the SAM database

- Creating and obtaining agreement for the detailed design documentation of all of the SAM processes, including process deliverables, interfaces, dependencies, measurements, metrics, KPIs and CSFs. The SAM processes should encompass all of the process areas described in Chapter 5
- Implementing the agreed SAM processes, together with process roles and responsibilities. This stage of the project may also involve the deployment and implementation of additional tools to facilitate the automation of the SAM processes wherever possible. This could be achieved using a 'big bang' deployment of the tools and processes but is much more likely to use some form of phased deployment throughout the organization (see Chapter 7)
- Managing roll-out of training and awareness of tools and processes
- Collecting and analysing all of the information on software assets and usage
- Reviewing software purchasing processes to ensure the best licensing terms, contracts and prices for software acquisition, and that all software is authentically purchased and properly registered both internally and externally with the software suppliers
- Preparing project progress reports and reviews
- Monitoring and reviewing all objectives, measurements, metrics, KPIs, and CSFs to ensure that the project has successfully met with all of its planned targets. This is the action that ensures you reach the 'desired state'
- Selecting, testing and deploying new or updated SAM tools
- Defining and agreeing on report content, structure, frequency and distribution

■ Conducting an end-of-project review and sign-off for each part of the overall iterative process. The lessons learnt can then be fed into the next project.

How do you know when you have got there? Consider the following questions:

■ Have all the implementation objectives been met?
■ Have all the project deliverables been signed off?
■ Have all of the business benefits been realized?
■ Have all the CSFs been achieved?
■ Has the 'desired state' been achieved?
■ Has the project been successfully signed off?
■ Do the processes work?

6.3 STAYING THERE

The momentum generated during the project needs to be maintained within normal processes to ensure that they do not stagnate or even regress. It is also essential that the SAM processes are institutionalized and incorporated to become part of 'everyone's everyday job'. Another key element of process success is to establish within each of the SAM processes a culture of continuous improvement, so that the processes continue to develop and mature even after the implementation project is complete. The following activities will achieve this:

■ Incorporate the new SAM changes and processes into job descriptions and roles throughout ICT and the business, making them part of 'everyone's everyday job'

■ Maintain the profile and momentum by establishing a process of continuous improvement in each of the SAM processes (the Deming cycle of 'Plan–Do–Check–Act')
■ Prevent complacency and regression within the process by continually reinforcing the SAM key messages and by incorporating SAM issues and polices into information provided to all new starters
■ Continue with the monitoring, measurement and review of all measurements, metrics and KPIs to ensure continued development of the maturity of processes and to ensure that SAM-related CSFs are met
■ Continuously emphasize the importance of the SAM processes to all ICT and business personnel.

How do you know when you are staying there? Consider the following questions:

■ Are SAM policies in place and are they adhered to?
■ Is an appreciation of SAM part of the overall organizational culture?
■ Is SAM information included in 'starter packs' and induction programmes for new starters?
■ Is the number of exceptions detected reducing?
■ Is the number of detected inaccuracies within the SAM database reducing?
■ Is a process of continuous improvement operational in all areas of SAM?

6.4 PROVING YOU ARE STAYING THERE

It is important that as well as preserving, if not improving, the quality of the SAM processes, time is spent proving that the processes are maintaining the necessary levels of quality, effectiveness, efficiency and protection required by the business and the organization. The only method of proving that standards and quality are being maintained is by continuously carrying out the following processes:

- Conducting regular internal reviews and audits, and comparing the results against previous review exercises (minimum once per year, depending on the effectiveness of procedures for accurate record-keeping and licence management)
- Conducting regular external reviews and audits, and comparing the results against previous exercises and industry standards and benchmarks
- Gaining and retaining accreditation and certification against industry 'best practice' and quality standards
- Occasionally completing surprise or ad hoc reviews and audits
- Developing and measuring metrics that demonstrate continuous improvement year on year
- Implementing processes and procedures to deal with and rectify all inefficiencies and non-compliances identified during reviews and audits.

How do you know when you can prove you can stay there? Consider the following questions:

- Have you got all of the information and records relating to all software assets?
- If a software manufacturer questions your licence compliance are you confident you can provide information to satisfy them?
- If you had an external audit are you confident you can provide all of the necessary licence information to satisfy the auditors?
- Have you had supplier checks and were they satisfactory or were there any non-conformances?
- Have you had external audits that gave positive feedback about your processes?
- Have all issues of non-conformance from an audit been rectified?
- Do your records match those of your suppliers/manufacturers?

Tools and technology

7

7 Tools and technology

The appropriate use of tools within SAM processes is fundamental to their success. This chapter considers the types of tool that are available to assist with the effective management of software assets and how they can be used. The tools selected by an organization depend on many factors including, in particular, the platforms and technology already in place and the overall management tool architecture.

There is no single tool that provides a complete SAM solution, therefore leading organizations use a SAM toolset to underpin and automate the SAM processes and activities wherever possible. Moreover, there are now few standalone SAM tools, because many SAM tools have been merged with other management tools, such as operations management or service management tools.

SAM tool requirements should not be considered in isolation, but should be considered in conjunction with the overall requirement for management tools within the whole of ICT. This will ensure that whatever tools are purchased for use within software asset management, the SAM-related processes can be integrated with other ICT management tools as part of an overall management architecture. Information on the selection and use of tools is also given in section 7 of *Service Design* (TSO, 2007).

It is important that before buying any tool, the right culture has been established within the organization, and that people's roles and responsibilities have been determined. Often the implementation of a tool fails because the culture

of the organization is wrong or the processes are over-engineered, too bureaucratic or are not practical for certain user groups.

> **Key message**
>
> Tools should not be selected without having a clear understanding of how they will fit in with the culture of the organization, and with the roles and responsibilities of the people involved. How they will be used also needs to be clear before selection, including the extent to which they fit existing processes, require changed processes, or require software customization. For most environments, more than one tool will be required and in-depth knowledge of their deployment requirements will be necessary in their selection.

Figure 7.1 gives an overview of the SAM technology architecture, including the major types of tool available. Each of these is separately discussed in this chapter. There are many other tools available to support and manage the ICT infrastructure, for example to cover other areas of ITIL such as capacity management and release and deployment management. A discussion of those tools is beyond the scope of this guide.

There is a technology dimension to the measures software manufacturers sometimes apply to try to ensure that their software is properly licensed and is used in accordance with its terms and conditions. Understanding the relevant issues can help end-users deal with these measures more effectively,

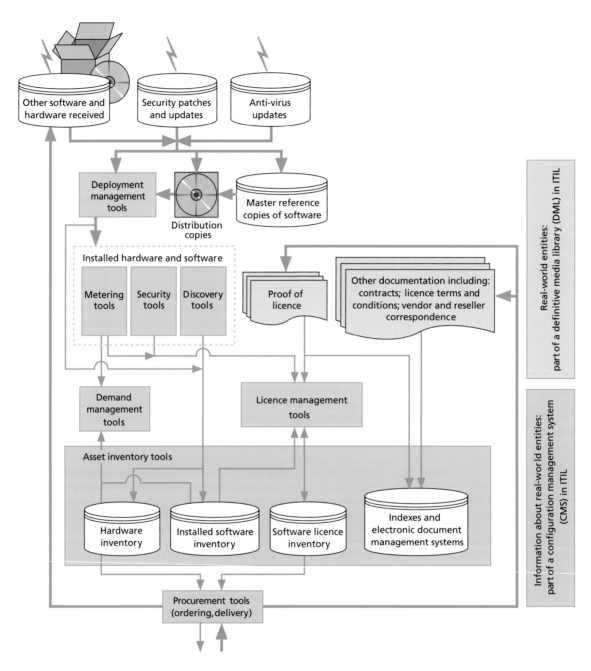

Figure 7.1 SAM technology architecture. Note that the figure is simplified. Thick arrows depict flows of software and physical assets. Thin arrows depict information flows.

and potentially gain additional value from them for internal purposes. These issues are discussed in section 7.10.

7.1 ASSET INVENTORY TOOLS

Asset inventory tools are the essential foundation of all SAM activity. At the simpler end of the spectrum, a spreadsheet may constitute the asset inventory tool for a small organization. However, a more extensive solution is usually to be expected.

Externally available software tools vary considerably in their functionality. At the top end, they are typically integrated with other functionality. Three broad categories of asset inventory functionality can be identified:

- **Inventories of hardware and installed software**   These are the most common types of tool, and are often integrated with, or designed to work with, discovery tools
- **Inventories of software licences**   Available functionality for managing software licences is comparatively limited. Tools for inventories of hardware and installed software may include some licence inventory functionality. There are also more specialist licence management applications available. Basic functionality includes the linking of different types of licence purchased to the current licences available for use, and where the use of the licence is assigned. Other functionality can support procurement functions including the reallocation of licences between different operational units
- **Document management systems**   Other physical documentation such as contracts and correspondence also needs to be managed and kept secure, as well as being made accessible.

Electronic document management systems are best suited to doing this, and allow easy linking or cross-referencing to other database systems. Copies of physical proof of licence would typically also be held in the document management system, with the originals stored in a separate, secure location.

7.2 DISCOVERY TOOLS

Discovery tools are designed to find hardware and installed software and collect relevant details about them. Discovery tools are used during an initial implementation, and also periodically during ongoing operations as part of the 'verification and audit' compliance process (see section 5.4.1).

A large number of tools in the market address this area. Some of the major issues involved are:

- **Platform**   Discovery tools need to be able to audit software on a range of platforms. Often an organization will have to use several different discovery tools because of the platform limitations of individual tools
- **Networked versus non-networked use**   Discovery tools are most efficient in a networked environment. However, there may be many machines that are seldom or never connected to a network, and methods must be found for getting information about these
- **Method and reliability of software identification**   There are several methods of software identification, and tools may provide for a combination of them. In general all approaches work well for major commercial applications developed and installed in accordance with industry standards. They are less helpful for in-house applications and much popular software commonly distributed via

the internet, such as file-swapping and instant messaging programs, which an organization may wish to identify and remove

- signatures – some discovery tools utilize 'signature' information about the names, sizes etc. of key files for particular applications. These tools depend on the signature files being updated to allow new software to be identified
- internal file documentation – well-designed commercial software following industry standards will now include internal fields that can be read by discovery software, without the need to have signature files. Programs that do not follow these standards will not be easily recognized
- registry entries – much software now also places entries in the system registry that can be read by discovery tools. Major commercial packages and installation routines do this. However, other types of software may not comply

■ **Ability to summarize meaningfully**   An application may consist of hundreds or thousands of individual files, all covered by one licence. Alternatively, a single licence may be required for one file. Installations may be complete or partial. Updates and patches may be applied, potentially affecting large numbers of files. Installations may be uninstalled, but without removing all of the relevant files. Discovery tools differ greatly in how user-friendly and accurate they are in identifying specific applications and the state of installation of each application. Extensive manual effort may be required to turn the output of discovery tools into meaningful summary application information.

The output from discovery tools is often used as the basis for licence compliance assessment. However, such an approach may give the wrong results without a full understanding of how software is actually used and the relevant licensing terms and conditions. For example, an application may be installed on a server, where it would be discovered only once. However, it might be executed from the server by many people connected to it, each of whom might require a licence.

7.3   METERING TOOLS

Metering tools or usage tools as they are sometimes referred to, are intended to measure active usage of a software product, rather than simply detect its existence as discovery tools do. When these tools are used just to monitor and report, they may be referred to as 'passive metering' tools. When they are used also to verify licences before running, they may be referred to as 'active metering' tools (especially for third-party products). Terminology used by different tools may vary. Many of the metering/usage tools often form part of an integrated toolset. Metering tools require the same type of regular metric/signature updating as discovery tools. Metering will only produce meaningful information for those applications it has been set up to recognize.

Metering tools are historically most closely associated with monitoring the usage of server-based applications. Some licences are sold with 'concurrent usage' rights, which means that there is a maximum number of people who can use the software at any one time. Metering tools can be effective at providing absolute control against available licences in these cases. Alternatively, when the maximum is exceeded, an exception condition can be generated to initiate corrective action or the purchasing of additional licences.

Metering tools are increasingly being used to measure active usage on non-server devices, especially workstations. Some tools can even distinguish between active and minimized applications. With appropriate analysis, active usage information can help identify software that is installed but which is not being used actively. Decisions may be taken to redeploy licences being unnecessarily tied up in this way, rather than purchase yet more licences when they are needed elsewhere.

Licence verification functionality has also developed considerably. In particular, there are now a number of third-party tools providing these capabilities, referred to as active metering tools. These capabilities may be largely standalone, or incorporated in broader suites of products.

A major consideration with metering tools is their performance overheads. Increasingly, there are also legal issues in countries where there are strong employee rights or workers' councils. In these countries, a metering tool may be considered as a way of controlling the individual. The exact type of metering to be implemented may need to be assessed carefully, and done in consultation with the appropriate employee representative organizations.

7.4 LICENCE MANAGEMENT TOOLS

Licence management tools are potentially among the most important tools in a SAM implementation. However, the state of the market is comparatively immature, although there have been some significant recent development of their functionality and capability. Licence management

is largely manual in many organizations, and prone to error or not being done at all. Automation, to the extent that it exists, is often just for the simpler types of software licensing and usage information, e.g. from discovery tools or from metering tools.

There are several types of functionality that may be considered necessary for a licence management tool:

- Being able to determine and track on a regular basis (without extensive manual work) the need for each type of licence, based on the appropriate usage criteria. For example, the need for licences may be based on: the number of installed copies; the total number of users; the maximum number of concurrent users; or the number of connected printers divided by five
- Being able to demonstrate the effective licences held, which requires the linking of upgrade licences with the underlying full original licences
- Being able to link licence requirements to effective licences held, and to report on licensing exceptions identified
- Being able to manage 'stocks' of unused licences, and potentially negative 'stocks' if licences only need to be ordered periodically after the software is installed
- Being able to facilitate the transfer of licences held to different operational units.

Ideally, licence management should be at the level of individual licences, linking specific licences to where those licences are used. Doing this may require linking different volume licences for different quantities of licences in complex ways.

7.5 CONTRACT MANAGEMENT TOOLS

Contract management information is likely to be integrated with licence management information, since many detailed licence management issues link in to overall contractual issues. It may also be integrated with financial purchasing software. The types of functionality needed in this area include:

■ Supplier and contracts database systems for the recording and management of contracts and suppliers as detailed in section 4.7 on supplier management in *Service Design* (TSO, 2007)

■ Warning about automatic contract extensions or maintenance payments due, deadlines for internally initiated renewals etc.

■ Monitoring total purchasing levels against agreements to ensure that relevant commitments or projections are being met, for pricing purposes.

(Contract management functionality is not shown in Figure 7.1.)

7.6 DEMAND MANAGEMENT TOOLS

Demand management can be viewed as an add-on capability for metering tools. The objective is to highlight software that is inactive, not being actively used over a given period, and for which it may be possible to save money by redeploying the underused licences.

7.7 DEPLOYMENT MANAGEMENT TOOLS

Deployment tool technology is comparatively well developed. The issue for SAM is to ensure that deployments are properly authorized, and that relevant deployment data is captured within the SAM database.

7.8 SECURITY TOOLS

There are several security issues that are particularly relevant to SAM, for which there are a number of tools available. There is considerable overlap between this area and that of security in general, and the two must be clearly coordinated for best results.

■ **Installation security tools**   There are a number of approaches to controlling software installations, and preventing unauthorized installations. Some of these can be implemented at the operating system level. There are also some major packages that have extensive functionality for determining who can install and/or run which software. (There may be other related SAM functionality included, such as metering)

■ **Protection tools**   Anti-virus software can be viewed as a SAM concern, as can general protection measures meant to protect existing software assets from compromise. The main issue for the rest of SAM is to ensure that anti-virus and security patch update procedures are tightly integrated into the overall process for software asset management, so that updates are distributed quickly and reliably when needed.

7.9 PROCUREMENT TOOLS

Procurement is an important area for SAM (see section 5.3.4). Increasingly, procurement tools and solutions are being developed that are targeted at SAM benefits. Relevant capabilities include:

■ Ability to check online for the availability of unused licences as part of the ordering process, checking initially within the immediate operating entity and then potentially with affiliated organizations that may have spare licences to transfer

■ Automatic linking of ordered licences to relevant licensee, e.g. PCs or individuals, to avoid repeat work later.

7.10 VENDOR LICENCE MANAGEMENT TECHNOLOGY

The focus of this guide is on customer management of software assets, including licensing. However, there are also a number of vendor (i.e. software manufacturer) technologies used directly by the manufacturer to help ensure proper licensing and use in accordance with terms and conditions. These may have infrastructure implications to ensure that the software continues to run.

■ **Licensing keys**   Licensing keys are the most widely used approach to vendor-managed use, and generally the least effective at preventing unlicensed use. However, it may be possible to trace the source of keys on unauthorized copies, especially if the keys are unique to individual licences. Unauthorized use may come to the attention of software manufacturers in many ways, such as technical support calls by users with problems, during internet connections to download updates and as a result of audits

■ **Hardware dongles**   This is one of the simplest secure forms of licence management technology, with each program keyed to require a specific hardware dongle to be attached to the PC (or other equipment) for it to run

■ **Technical licence management**   With this technology, electronic licence certificates are obtained centrally and distributed to individual PCs, users etc. as required. The product itself checks to see if the licence is available. Vendors may implement this type of technology to handle different architectures and build in flexibility for unlicensed use, e.g. granting a grace period before enforcement, or allowing a grace period if there is a licence certificate interruption. A licence server is usually required, either online for each execution or to provide a more permanent key that may be used when not connected.

■ **Metering**   With this technology, the licensed product itself does no checking, but rather an independent monitoring agent identifies its (requested) execution and can record usage and also prevent execution. There are many ways of bypassing this type of control, which may be partially addressed by protected logs that can be analysed, e.g. for completeness of time coverage

■ **Wrapper technology**   This technology encapsulates an application that cannot otherwise be controlled by technical licence management, so that the wrapper provides this functionality. The wrapper technology may impact on the maintainability of the product, e.g. the ability or the amount of time and work required to implement patches.

Partners and software asset management

8

8 Partners and software asset management

'Partner' is used here in the sense of organizations involved in a (potential) business relationship or association. This chapter highlights some of the ways that an organization may use partners to support SAM implementations and ongoing SAM operations. Many of these possibilities are not generally recognized or understood. They may be significant factors in determining the ease with which SAM is implemented and operates.

In general, references are not made to any particular partners or sources. It is possible to find current information about many of these areas by using a good internet search engine and entering key words or phrases such as 'software asset management', or by going to the websites of major partners of any of the types listed below.

The comments in this section are subjective, but are intended to give practical advice based on experienced views. There will be exceptions to the generalizations given here. Furthermore, the market will continue to develop, meaning that some of these comments will become obsolete over time.

The types of partner covered here are:

- Software manufacturers/vendors
- Resellers
- SAM tool vendors and implementers
- SAM consultants
- SAM outsourcers
- Auditors
- IT research organizations
- Professional and industry associations
- Anti-piracy organizations.

Many partner organizations fulfil more than one of these roles. Suggested criteria for selecting partners are given in Appendix D.

The main types of deliverable available from partners are:

- SAM guidance materials, including 'best-practice' guidelines
- SAM consultancy
- Outsourcing of SAM functions
- Audits
- Certification
- Conferences and workshops
- Licensing advice
- Historical purchase records and effective licensing
- Current purchase records
- Directories and assessments of SAM tools
- SAM tools
- Implementation assistance for SAM tools.

Each of these is discussed in more detail below, concluding with a discussion of the special considerations for reseller relationships.

8.1 SAM GUIDANCE MATERIALS

A number of guides are available about SAM, especially over the internet from software manufacturers and anti-piracy organizations. Much of the focus is on licensing compliance issues for smaller organizations rather than on the broader issues of comprehensive SAM.

Research organizations publish overview materials about various issues related to SAM, such as trends in the SAM tool marketplace and issues related to total cost of ownership.

8.2 SAM CONSULTANCY

At the time of writing this guide, SAM consultancy industry-wide is in its comparative infancy, but the area is developing quickly and is creating some of the 'best practice' described in this guide. Concerns about licence compliance drive much of this work. There is also a consultancy approach driven from the strategic procurement side, which tends to focus on quick wins in procurement arrangements and not on longer-term infrastructure projects. The most in-depth consultancy projects are generally associated with tool implementation.

SAM consultancy tends to be provided by highly experienced individuals, typically operating in small organizations or in small units of large organizations. Assessing the qualifications and suitability of a potential SAM consultant is not straightforward. See Appendix D for suggestions about how to approach this.

8.3 OUTSOURCING OF SAM FUNCTIONS

Different types of outsourcing related to SAM are available, such as:

- Application service provider (ASP)-type hosting and maintenance of specialist licence management applications
- Capture of orders via an external provider order-entry application placed on the end-customer's intranet, linked to the reseller systems

- Full ICT procurement processing via implants within an organization, e.g. the ICT procurement function may be largely subcontracted to a specialist team from an outsourcer, but operating fully within the user organization
- Ongoing responsibility for full ICT asset discovery and inventory, to provide regularly updated information about ICT assets both to local management and to corporate management.

Outsourcing may be one of the fastest, most reliable and most cost-effective ways of achieving SAM objectives. However, careful management is important as in all outsourcing situations. Some of the issues to consider are:

- Who has responsibility for ensuring licence compliance and for handling the costs of possible licence compliance audits required by software manufacturers? (Legally, how effectively can the responsibility for licence compliance ever be passed to a third party, and what operational responsibilities therefore can be delegated appropriately?)
- Possible conflicts with other outsourcers and internal units in protection of perceived 'territories'
- Possible conflicts of interest from the outsourcer, e.g. unwillingness to move to new technology or systems, or to improve problem areas, because of potential revenue impact or inflexible contracts. Also possible conflicts of interest if the outsourcer performs other functions, e.g. if it is a reseller
- Establishing e-monitoring service levels.

8.4 AUDITS

Effective SAM cannot be achieved without auditing the machines hosting the software. Furthermore, a snapshot or one-off audit does not provide ongoing compliance. A continuous process is required to maintain control of the asset base.

The main types of audit related to SAM concern licence compliance. These may be conducted by:

- Software manufacturers directly
- Independent third-party organizations on behalf of software organizations. Most often, independent accountancy firms are engaged by software manufacturers to conduct audits of licence compliance. (Many volume-licensing agreements specifically provide for this.) These reviews may be invoked under the audit clauses of relevant licensing agreements, but more often they are mutually agreed with the end-user organization and structured to provide coverage of broader SAM issues than just licence compliance. These reviews focus on the software of the software manufacturer
- Independent third-party organizations on behalf of end-user organizations. A broad range of organizations (e.g. resellers, consultants, auditors) provide licensing audits directly for end-user organizations. These reviews tend to cover a broad range of software and hardware assets. They may be initiated based on pure internal requirements, as the result of a perceived risk of external review, or in connection with certification programmes in some countries
- Internal auditors or quality management personnel.

Section 8.5 deals with the subject of certification audits.

8.5 CERTIFICATION

There are many types of certification available that relate to SAM, but their profile is relatively low. These are addressed in the following sections.

8.5.1 SAM and licence compliance certifications

There are a small number of certification programmes around the world for licence compliance or SAM. These have generally been offered by or in association with software manufacturers or anti-piracy organizations. Such certifications at present have little legal weight. Their primary value is internal, to demonstrate a level of accomplishment in achieving SAM goals.

SAM and licence compliance certification programmes are appealing in principle, but they have some limitations:

- There have been no generally agreed standards for assessment of good SAM performance, until the emergence of ISO/IEC 19770, and this standard is now gaining wide acceptance and recognition within the industry
- Certification prior to the emergence of the ISO/IEC 19770 standard, had particular value to an organization if it meant no manufacturer licensing audits for a period of time. However, this could have been viewed as giving carte blanche for new licensing breaches for the entire period of certification, so manufacturers were wary of it. The wording on the certificates was therefore typically carefully limited
- Certification is only as good as the skills of the certifiers, and for the areas covered.

Example

A subsidiary of a multinational organization obtained certification of its SAM systems from an anti-piracy organization. The subsidiary was then audited by a software manufacturer and found to be substantially under-licensed. The subsidiary had good administrative systems, but it did not properly understand the terms of its organization's global licensing agreements and had not purchased necessary licences.

8.5.2 Personal certifications

There are now personal qualifications and certifications based on the contents of this SAM guide and the ISO 19770 SAM standard. The two principal qualifications in this area are:

■ Certificate in Software Asset Management Essentials: this qualification provides an introduction to the SAM processes as described in this publication and also provides details of the interdependencies between SAM and the IT service management processes

■ Practitioner Certificate in Software Asset Management: this qualification provides software asset managers, working in medium to large companies, with the knowledge to implement and maintain an effective SAM programme.

These courses are available from a number of training providers worldwide.

Also, the anti-piracy side of one industry software organization has offered a personal qualification in software asset management based on a short course and exam. Personal certifications are also available in a number of ICT areas that impact on SAM, from various sources.

Personal certifications may also be available from software manufacturers for their own licensing programmes. These are generally intended for reseller personnel, but it is worth an end-user organization asking if these are available for its personnel as well.

8.5.3 General procedural certifications

There are various national and international standards such as ISO 9001 that may be relevant to SAM. Each standards body has its own arrangements for awarding the certifications. The main limitations of such certifications for software asset management purposes at present are:

■ The scope of procedures covered does not have to include much, if anything, related to SAM

■ To the extent that SAM-related processes may be covered, there is little basis for the assessment of the adequacy of the procedures documented, but rather only compliance to them. As a result, certification may indicate compliance with poorly designed procedures.

For specific review of the SAM processes and their effectiveness, the organizational processes can be compared against the requirements and outcomes documented in Part 1 of the ISO/IEC 19770 SAM standard.

8.6 CONFERENCES AND WORKSHOPS

Professional and industry associations and research organizations are good sources of conferences and workshops addressing SAM or related issues. Almost all of the other types of partner also tend to stage conferences and workshops. These may be good opportunities for getting ideas and talking to people who have gone through the process of implementing SAM.

8.7 LICENSING ADVICE

Good licensing advice is a major factor in achieving licensing savings. Ultimately, the end-user organization has the responsibility for its own licensing, so it cannot place excessive reliance on external advice. Nonetheless, having good external sources of licensing advice is an important aide in recognizing opportunities and minimizing exposure.

Software manufacturers may offer detailed written guidance on their own licensing issues and this is often available on their website.

Overall, resellers are probably the best source of consistently accessible detailed licensing advice, although the variability in quality is great. When assessing a reseller (or other organization) for its licensing advice, the rate of turnover of licensing specialist personnel should be considered. It is also a good idea to ask some detailed questions to see how well they can advise on specific licensing issues, and compare answers between different resellers. A good reseller will identify areas where money can be saved.

Example

One reseller advised a customer that the order they were placing for a major infrastructure upgrade was not required, because previously purchased upgrade insurance (forgotten by the customer) already provided the necessary upgrade rights.

Good resellers know the detailed considerations of software licensing conditions because they are experienced and specialize in these aspects, dealing with them on a daily basis.

8.8 HISTORICAL PURCHASE RECORDS AND EFFECTIVE LICENSING

For any organization undertaking a SAM implementation, a major challenge is to determine what licences are already owned, because of historical problems of poor retention of proof of licence, and poor filing of old invoices.

Software manufacturers may be able to provide detailed information about historical purchases through volume-licensing programmes, for which the manufacturer normally records the name of the purchaser. The success of this approach will depend on the size of the requesting organization, the specific manufacturer involved, sometimes on the geographical location of the manufacturer's office, and on the ease of identifying the records for the organization that may have had name and organizational changes. (The names recorded on licensing records may be highly arbitrary depending on what the purchaser wrote down.) Nonetheless, this is one of the best potential sources of historical licensing information for most large organizations undertaking a SAM implementation. Having a copy of software manufacturer historical purchasing records will go some way towards addressing the problem of a lack of proof of licence for historical purchases. These purchase records do not constitute proof of licence, but it is unlikely that a software manufacturer would take legal action about licences it knew had been purchased.

There may be problems in making use of such data if there have been large-scale mergers or demergers. In such cases, a major exercise may be required to analyse the deployment and movement of licences over time, and to produce formal licence transfer documentation to regularize the situation. The value of licences found through such an exercise is typically much higher than an organization will know by itself at the beginning of a SAM implementation.

Software manufacturers might also be able to provide an 'effective licensing' analysis of purchase records. This is an analysis of the different types of licence purchased, including upgrades and upgrade insurance, to determine the current effective licences that are owned, after all upgrades are applied to the respective underlying products.

Resellers may also be able to provide detailed information about historical purchases. The typical advantages of getting such information from resellers are:

- The data is often at a lower level of organizational detail than the manufacturer holds, allowing for better historical analysis and subsequent tracking
- The data covers all products sold by that reseller, not just a single software manufacturer.

The typical disadvantages are:

- Often the data will not be available because the reseller has gone out of business, or systems have been converted leaving old data inaccessible
- The reseller may not be cooperative if it is no longer a major supplier to the organization requesting the information
- The records have less credibility with the software manufacturer and potentially in court
- The information might be provided in a completely different format incompatible with existing information.

This third point is seldom stressed, but is important, because resellers may not always sell authentic products, or may not (accidentally or intentionally)

report orders through to the manufacturer for volume licences. This is why a proof of licence produced by the manufacturer itself is always so important. In any case, it is worth asking the reseller for its data download. Any information obtained will almost always be useful, even if manufacturer data is also obtained, because of the additional reseller order detail compared with the manufacturer's information.

Some resellers, consultants and tool implementers might also be able to provide 'effective licensing' analyses of the licences purchased by an organization, based on historical purchasing records. Typically, this would be a charged service.

The time and cost to retrieve and analyse historical purchase records could potentially be quite high. Therefore, an assessment should be made of the expected value of the licences that will be identified in this way, against the cost of performing the exercise.

8.9   CURRENT PURCHASE RECORDS

Regardless of the situation with historical purchase records, an organization can benefit from arrangements to have access to current purchase records. These abilities depend significantly on the manufacturer and on the reseller, with a spectrum of different capabilities being available.

In some cases, online access is now available to manufacturers' systems to see current purchasing transactions. These systems may also provide proof of licence. This online customer access to manufacturers' records has proved very useful in licence management even in the absence of a more extensive SAM approach.

Resellers can also offer extensive capabilities in this area. Larger resellers, in particular, can offer larger organizations with multiple locations a way to allow decentralized ordering, but clear visibility from the centre of all purchasing activity, for all software manufacturers and also for hardware – as long as the decentralized locations use these facilities. These reporting facilities may also be associated with specialized order entry interfaces.

Some resellers can also offer a download capability into in-house SAM systems for recording all licences purchased, for use in licence management.

8.10 DIRECTORIES AND ASSESSMENTS OF SAM TOOLS

There is only a limited amount of information available about SAM tools. ICT research organizations provide some, including useful information about market trends and possible vendors' viability problems. There is also currently at least one major directory of SAM tools available from a software manufacturer's website. Additional information on the selection of SAM tools is contained in Appendix B.

There are also directories of tools available for other functionalities of ITIL. For example, at the time of writing of this guide, there is such a directory on the website of the British Computer Society Configuration Management Specialist Group (www.bcs-cmsg.org.uk).

8.11 SAM TOOLS

There are hundreds of tools with some sort of SAM capability, but in practice a more limited number of tools are used widely for 'production' in larger organizations. Such tools may be identified by discussion with other organizations and with consultants, by web searches, and in directories as indicated above.

There are also a significant number of 'discovery' tools more readily available, sometimes for free download in their complete versions or for trial. The websites of manufacturers and of anti-piracy organizations are good places to check. Manufacturer discovery tools can be expected to cover at least that manufacturer's own software reasonably well.

Some SAM solutions exist that integrate the order process with an internal licence management system, to ensure that licences are not purchased unless needed. Some resellers can also offer specialized order placement interfaces. Typically this is by means of an internet-based ordering application that ensures that the products being ordered are currently available from the manufacturer, and authorized for the customer (e.g. available under the customer's purchasing contract). See also Chapter 7.

8.12 IMPLEMENTATION ASSISTANCE FOR SAM TOOLS

Implementation assistance for SAM tools may be offered by tool manufacturers themselves, especially for the largest enterprise systems, or for much smaller manufacturers. However, assistance for many of the mid-range and longer-established SAM tools is often provided by consultancy organizations, including resellers.

8.13 SPECIAL CONSIDERATIONS FOR RESELLER RELATIONSHIPS

This section is written with the explicit knowledge of a large number of reseller and customer audits.

Software assets are complex assets to control for the organization. They are not like pencils that can be bought in bulk and left on the shelf with little worry. Likewise, the reseller of software assets needs to have special skills, and, as an organization starts to recognize the importance of software assets and of SAM, the importance of having a good reseller will be increasingly recognized.

Unfortunately, the focus of many procurement departments is primarily on price. Resellers competing for this trade cut margins paper-thin, and can become essentially nothing more than order-processing back offices. If the customer is fully on top of all licensing matters, that is fine. However, this is not the standard situation. The customer then has a significant risk of not recognizing both major opportunities and major risks related to software assets. A factual observation is that there are many breakdowns in reseller processes in these situations, and many licensing problems encountered by customers. For example, a reseller may price software low, with the expectation of getting profit on related services. But the software sales unit will not be able to justify building good logistical systems or keeping skilled licensing personnel. The customer will be encouraged to do things that keep reseller processing costs low – such as consolidating orders – which make SAM more difficult to achieve for the customer. The selection of a reseller should be based on more than price. A marginally higher cost should be more than offset by the benefits of better service and better licensing advice.

Mapping SAM to ITIL and other approaches

9

9 Mapping SAM to ITIL and other approaches

There are many different approaches that can be used to manage, support and deliver ICT services to the organization. Some are based on proprietary architectures and frameworks, others are based on open, non-proprietary standards and best-practice guidelines. The three leading open guidelines and standards in this area are:

- The OGC's IT infrastructure library (ITIL)
- The ISO 20000 (ISO/IEC 20000)
- The IT Governance Institute's Control Objectives for Information and related Technology (COBIT).

The following sections give a brief outline of SAM relationships to these open guidelines and standards, together with some of the major proprietary management standards. The key area within all of these standards is that of asset and configuration management. The scope of these processes differs within these standards/guidelines:

- In ITIL, the responsibility principally lies within the service asset and configuration management (SACM), release and deployment management and financial management processes
- In ISO/IEC 20000, the responsibility also principally lies within the configuration management, release management and financial management processes
- In COBIT, the responsibility principally lies within the processes of 'Manage the IT Investment' and 'Manage the Configuration'.

In organizations where these processes are less well developed and integrated, it is possible that there is duplication of effort between the various processes or more likely, and more dangerously, gaps between the individual processes. In order for these processes to be successful within the organization, these aspects of SAM should form part of the overall strategies and plans of the ICT unit.

> **Key message**
>
> It is imperative that there is end-to-end continuity and integration between the various constituent SAM processes, whether an organization is based on ITIL, ISO/IEC 20000 or COBIT principles and guidelines.

The discussion of these issues and the mapping of SAM processes to these different approaches are considered in detail within the following sections.

9.1 SAM AND ITIL

One of the most comprehensive guidelines on the management of IT services is contained within ITIL. This is a library containing a distillation of 'best-practice' guidelines on the processes involved in the management, support and delivery of quality ICT services.

A high-level mapping of SAM to ITIL is given in section 1.11. This section gives additional detail about such a mapping by reference to more detailed ITIL information. The management of asset and configuration information is seen principally as part of the role of the Service Transition and Service Operation stages of the lifecycle, although SAM interfaces to all stages of the lifecycle.

SACM is one of the primary Service Transition processes and is of major significance to software asset management. SACM manages not only the assets and their associated lifecycles, but also the links and relationships between the assets. It also includes the management of relationships between these assets and other service management-related issues such as incidents, problems and changes, services and SLAs.

Management of the physical software assets of an organization is also considered to be one of the key roles of SACM. Thus, the control of the media, licence and authenticity documentation is all part of the remit of this process. (All of the financial aspects of asset management are within the scope of financial management, discussed separately below.)

Asset management within SAM is all of these aspects together. Asset management, however, forms the basis of any good SAM system, and is best accomplished using a supporting relational database. The overall asset management processes within SAM include:

- Management of all aspects of software assets
- Management of the associated hardware assets, to the extent necessary for SAM
- Control and management of software components through all of the stages of their lifecycle
- Management of software authenticity documentation and licences
- Management of procurement and software contractual documentation
- Storage and management of all master software media
- Control and management of all installed copies of software
- Management of the relationships between all of the above aspects
- The periodic reconciliation of the contents of the DML with the contents of the configuration management system (CMS) with what is in use in the 'real-world' live environment.

Figure 9.1 illustrates the relationships between the DML containing the physical software assets themselves together with the licence and contractual information and the CMS containing the logical information as a part of an overall service knowledge management system (SKMS).

In Figure 9.1, the dashed lines indicate the movement and deployment of physical components, which is the responsibility of the release and deployment process, whereas the solid lines indicate the logical links and relationships contained within the CMS, which is the responsibility of SACM. The design, development and implementation of these aspects of the process are crucial to the operation of efficient processes for the management of software assets. Within ITIL, each component contained within the CMS is referred to as a configuration item (CI). Each CI record within the CMS contains all of the attributes and information relating to a component necessary for managing it, whether software, hardware, contracts etc.

The DML acts as a single logical storage repository for all master copies of software in live use, or planned to be in live use within the organization.

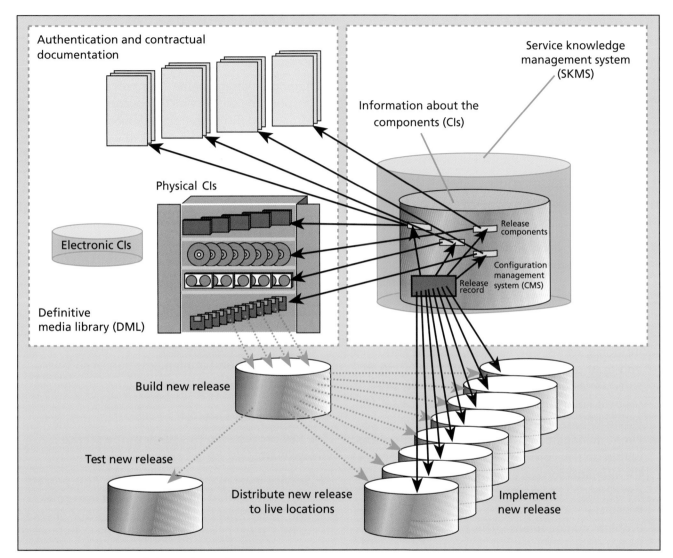

Figure 9.1 ITIL use of the DML and CMS

Only quality-controlled software that has successfully completed all appropriate quality assurance checks should be registered and stored within the DML. All authenticity and licence documentation should also be stored within the DML. Scanned copies of these may also be stored within the CMS. Within ITIL, the responsibility for the DML resides within the SACM process. This is also a fundamental requirement of good SAM processes. Generally, source code versions of in-house software are stored within the DML, whereas for bought-in software executable versions are stored.

Within ITIL, SACM is the critical process in the support of SAM. The relationships between the other lifecycle stages and areas of ITIL and SAM are illustrated in Figure 1.2. The other main areas of ITIL that also provide important support of SAM are described below.

9.1.1 Service Operation

The key processes in this stage of the service lifecycle are:

- **Service desk, incident management and request fulfilment management** These areas are responsible within an ITIL conformant organization for the provision of a single point of contact for all users of ICT services and systems. Between them, they manage all incidents, issues, queries, requests and enquiries and must ensure that all anomalies relating to software assets, licences and their usage are reported immediately to the SAM processes for resolution and rectification or escalation
- **Event management** This process is responsible within an ITIL conformant organization for the management of all types of event and can provide vital support for effective SAM processes
- **Problem management** This process is responsible within an ITIL conformant organization for the analysis of the root cause of incidents and problems and their subsequent prevention. SAM should work with problem management to ensure that all SAM exceptions are analysed to proactively prevent their recurrence.

9.1.2 Service Transition

In addition to the SACM process, the other key processes in this stage of the service lifecycle are:

- **Change management** This process is responsible within an ITIL conformant organization for the management and control of all changes within an ICT environment. All changes involving software should be analysed for their impact on the SAM processes. They should then be managed through the stages of their lifecycle to ensure that all requirements of the SAM processes are satisfied, especially with regard to licence compliance and updating of the CMS. The operation of an effective change management process is crucial to successful SAM processes
- **Release and deployment management** This process is responsible within an ITIL conformant organization for the physical control, deployment and implementation of software into the live environment.

9.1.3 Service Design

The key processes in this stage of the service lifecycle are:

- **Service level management (SLM)** This process must ensure that all customer and user roles and responsibilities are agreed and documented within SLAs. Conditions must be included within all SLAs detailing that all users of ICT systems must accept, agree, sign and abide by the organization's policies on software, security and internet usage, before using ICT systems and accessing ICT services
- **Availability management** This process should be involved where any software assets are

responsible for causing service or component availability or unavailability issues

- **IT service continuity management (ITSCM)** This process would need to ensure that all recovery and continuity plans are in place for all software in use within the organization. Therefore, SAM processes should inform ITSCM of all new or changed software. Also ITSCM should ensure that all SAM issues have been addressed on all standby and recovery sites and systems
- **Information security management** This process would assist with the assessment of risk and the implementation of mitigation actions and countermeasures. Security management should also assist with the detection, alerting and escalation of all software exceptions and non-compliance
- **Supplier management** This process would assist with the management of all aspects of contractual and supplier issues associated with software, software partners and vendors.

9.1.4 Service Strategy

The SAM strategy should form an essential part of the overall organizational service strategy. The sourcing of software and the selection of software partners are key elements of the overall strategy of the ICT organization.

The other key strategic area is **financial management**. This area is responsible for the management and control of all ICT-related finances and costs. Details of all software procurement and actual expenditure should be collected and analysed by financial management, including all support and maintenance contracts, for incorporation into financial cost models.

9.1.5 Continual Service Improvement

This stage of the lifecycle should provide a framework and approach to the continual improvement of the SAM processes. It is essential that SAM is seen as a key and integrated part of the effective measurement and improvement of service management processes.

9.2 SAM AND ISO/IEC 20000

The ISO/IEC 20000 standard is closely aligned with ITIL. Therefore the interfaces and dependencies that SAM has with the various processes involved are similar to many of those within ITIL. They are split into five separate areas:

- **Service delivery processes** These are very similar in content to many of the Service Design processes within ITIL, but also additionally include the service reporting process. They principally concern the delivery and improvement of quality of ICT service delivered to the business
- **Control processes** These consist of configuration management and change management
- **Release processes** The release management process is the only process within this area
- **Resolution processes** These consist of incident management and problem management processes
- **Relationship processes** These consist of the relationship management processes relating to supplier and business relationship management.

The control, release and resolution processes are similar to the equivalent ITIL Service Transition and Service Operation processes involved in the day-to-day support and maintenance of ICT services and systems and the transition of new services.

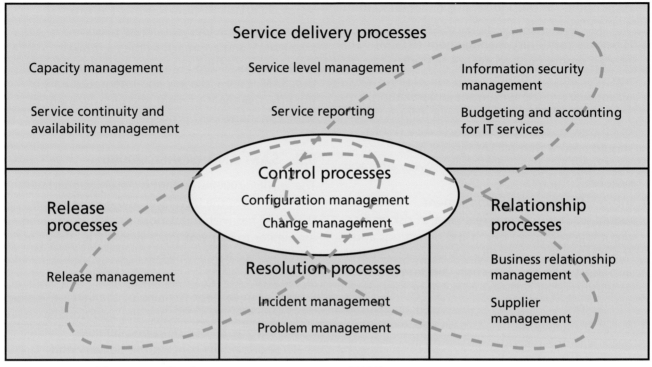

Figure 9.2 Relationship between SAM and the ISO/IEC 20000 service management processes. Redrawn from ISO/IEC 20000 standard with the permission of ISO

The principal areas of ISO/IEC 20000 that interface with SAM are the service delivery, control, release and relationship processes as illustrated in Figure 9.2, with the major areas being covered by the configuration, change and release management processes. Within ISO/IEC 20000, responsibility for the CMS, the DML and the physical management of the media, licensing and authenticity documentation is all within the configuration and release management processes.

Release management is also responsible for the physical control and distribution of all software and hardware assets throughout the organization, which is also a fundamental component of

the SAM processes. It is essential that release management only distributes authentic software throughout the organization for operational use and that relevant licences exist for all operational copies.

The budgeting and accounting process within the service delivery area of ISO/IEC 20000 also performs key financial elements of the SAM process functionality. The roles of the other processes within the service delivery processes, the resolution processes and control processes of ISO/IEC 20000 are similar to their ITIL equivalents.

ISO/IEC 20000 also includes the area of relationship processes, consisting of the business relationship and supplier management processes. These also perform significant elements of the SAM process requirements.

- **Business relationship management (BRM)** This endeavours to establish and maintain good relationships with the business. It should involve educating the customers and ensuring that they understand their role within the SAM processes. Everyone within the organization is responsible for complying with all of the policies relating to the use of ICT systems and services. It is BRM's role to develop a culture where this is understood and these policies are adhered to throughout the business
- **Supplier management** This is the management of all suppliers including software suppliers, partners and resellers. In terms of SAM requirements, this process must guarantee that only reputable and responsible software suppliers are used to ensure that only authentic software is procured and that subsequently licences are secured from the actual software manufacturers. All interfaces and procedures with the suppliers should also be documented and adhered to.

9.3 SAM AND ISO/IEC 19770

The ISO/IEC 19770 Part 1 standard is very consistent with and is very closely aligned with the SAM processes contained within this publication. The processes within the ISO standard are contained in three main areas:

- **Organizational management processes for SAM** The objectives of these processes is to:

  - establish and maintain the management system within which the other SAM processes are implemented
  - ensure the effective and efficient accomplishment of SAM management objectives
- **Core SAM processes** The objective of these processes is to:
  - create and maintain all stores and records for software and related assets, and to provide the data management functionality which ensures the integrity of control of software and related assets in other SAM processes
  - detect and manage all exceptions to SAM policies, processes and procedures, including licence use rights
  - execute operational management functions that are essential to achieving overall SAM objectives and benefits
- **Primary process interfaces for SAM** The objective of this part of ISO/IEC 19770 is to:
  - specify SAM requirements for the lifecycle processes.

Figure 9.3 illustrates these three main areas and the processes within each of the areas.

The SAM standard is closely aligned with both ISO/IEC 20000 and this SAM publication. It has been developed to enable an organization to demonstrate that it is performing SAM at a level to satisfy corporate governance requirements and ensure effective support for IT service management processes and activities. It contains a set of requirements or a baseline for an integrated set of SAM processes as illustrated in Figure 9.3.

The standard defines an objective and a set of outcomes for each process, which are readily

Organizational management processes for SAM			
Control environment for SAM			
Corporate governance processes for SAM	Roles and responsibilities for SAM	Policies, processes and procedures for SAM	Competence in SAM
Planning and implementing processes for SAM			
Planning for SAM	Implementation of SAM	Monitoring and review of SAM	Continual improvement of SAM

Core SAM processes			
Inventory processes for SAM			
Software asset identification	Software asset inventory management	Software asset control	
Verification and compliance processes for SAM			
Software asset record verification	Software licensing compliance	Software asset security compliance	Conformance verification for SAM
Operation management processes and interfaces for SAM			
Relationship and contract management for SAM	Financial management for SAM	Service level management for SAM	Security management for SAM

Primary process interfaces for SAM			
Lifecycle process interfaces for SAM			
Change management process	Software development process	Software deployment process	Problem management process
Acquisition process	Software release management process	Incident management process	Retirement process

Figure 9.3 The ISO/IEC 19770 SAM processes

assessable. The standard does not include any information on the activities required to achieve the specified outcomes. This SAM guide contains details of the process and activities needed to deliver those outcomes. So in essence the ISO/IEC 19770 standard contains 'What' you need for effective SAM processes, whereas this publication contains 'How' the process should do it. So they can be used as a complementary set of documents establishing effective SAM processes within an organization.

9.4   SAM AND COBIT

COBIT (Copyright 1996, 1998, 2000, 2007, from the IT Governance Institute™) provides guidance on good practices for the management of IT processes in a manageable and logical structure (Figure

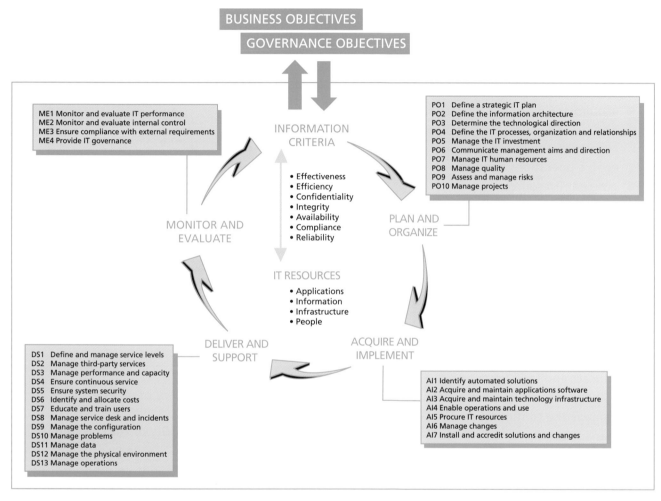

Figure 9.4 The COBIT framework

9.4). It has been produced by auditors as a set of processes and measures for the governance of ICT systems.

The 34 processes of COBIT are grouped into four separate domains as illustrated in Figure 9.4. These areas and processes are as follows:

■ **Plan and organize:**
  ● define a strategic IT plan
  ● define the information architecture
  ● determine the technological direction
  ● define the IT processes, organization and relationships
  ● manage the IT investment
  ● communicate management aims and direction
  ● manage IT human resources

- manage quality
- assess and manage risks
- manage projects
- **Acquire and implement:**
  - identify automated solutions
  - acquire and maintain applications software
  - acquire and maintain technology infrastructure
  - enable operations and use
  - procure IT resources
  - manage changes
  - install and accredit solutions and changes
- **Deliver and support:**
  - define and manage service levels
  - manage third-party services
  - manage performance and capacity
  - ensure continuous service
  - ensure system security
  - identify and allocate costs
  - educate and train users
  - manage service desk and incidents
  - manage the configuration
  - manage problems
  - manage data
  - manage the physical environment
  - manage operations
- **Monitor and evaluate:**
  - monitor and evaluate IT performance
  - monitor and evaluate internal control
  - ensure compliance with external requirements
  - provide IT governance.

Because the functionality of ICT management has been separated out into so many different processes, elements of SAM are covered in many more areas than is the case with either ITIL or ISO/

IEC 20000. These processes occur within all four domains of COBIT. However, the most significant SAM process within COBIT is that of 'manage the configuration'. The goals of this process are set out in the following box.

> **Manage the configuration**
>
> The goals of 'manage the configuration' are:
>
> - Optimize the IT infrastructure, resources and capabilities
> - Account for and protect all IT assets.

This process of 'manage the configuration' is a component of the 'deliver and support' domain within COBIT. It is one of the essential elements of COBIT and provides the basis for the operation of many of the other processes. It is very closely aligned with the SACM process of ITIL and the configuration management process of ISO/IEC 20000. The process within COBIT includes:

- Establishing a repository of all assets and configuration attributes and baselines
- Maintaining the integrity of the configuration repository
- Reviewing actual asset configurations for compliance with baselines within the repository.

Clearly the above activities are consistent with SAM processes and requirements. Another major area of COBIT responsible for significant aspects of SAM processes is 'manage the IT investment', within the 'plan and organize' domain. The key goals of this process are ensuring funding and controlling the disbursement of financial resources. The process is responsible for investment decisions, approving all expenditure and the recording and calculation of all costs associated with ICT systems and services.

Another relevant process within regard to SAM is that of 'ensure compliance with external requirements' within the 'monitor and evaluate' domain. The aim of this process is meeting legal, regulatory and contractual obligations and must ensure that all the necessary polices and procedures to achieve this have been documented, communicated and are regularly audited internally for compliance.

As can be seen from the lists of COBIT processes, there are many other areas that cover aspects of SAM processes, but the above are the key areas of COBIT with respect to SAM.

9.5 SAM AND OTHER MANAGEMENT FRAMEWORKS AND GUIDELINES

Several other frameworks and guidelines have been developed for the management of ICT services and systems. These have principally been developed by hardware or software manufacturer and supplier organizations. Examples of these are:

- **HP**, with its IT service management (ITSM) reference model
- **IBM**, with its IT Process Model (ITPM) framework
- **Microsoft**, with its Microsoft Operations Framework (MOF) guidelines
- **Sun**, with its Suntone framework.

These frameworks and guidelines have principally been based on or aligned with the ITIL framework and therefore the interactions between SAM and these frameworks have not been considered in further detail within this guide.

Appendix A: Software licensing overview

A

Appendix A: Software licensing overview

Software licensing is complex. Compliance with all of its terms and conditions requires in-depth knowledge. Typically, an organization will need to assign the responsibility for understanding licensing to specific individuals, and then ensure that they have the necessary training (initial and ongoing) to master the area.

This guide cannot act as a substitute to an organization understanding its own licensing terms and conditions. However, this appendix is intended to give the flavour of the complexity that can be found in software licensing.

Note: All comments in this section are generic, and may not correspond to specific terms and conditions of particular software.

A.1   WHEN LICENCES ARE REQUIRED

Software licences are rights to use software, with certain terms and conditions attached, and are one of the main issues addressed by software asset management. These rights to use software are totally separate from the legal rights to the software itself, which are normally kept by the software manufacturer or other third party. Licences may be bought, or may be 'free' subject to special terms and conditions. Even 'open-source' software normally has a licence, even though payment may not be required.

Licences are normally required whenever externally sourced software is 'used', which will typically be defined either as being installed on a machine, or as being executed on a machine, even if installed elsewhere (e.g. a server). They may also be defined in 'enterprise' terms, such as number of workstations or employees, in which case a licence is required for each qualifying unit or individual regardless of actual 'usage'.

Even with commercial software, there are several situations where paid licences may not be required, depending on specific contractual conditions. Often, these situations are not understood and, as a result, organizations may purchase licences they do not need. These situations include: workstations used for dedicated training purposes (with limits on numbers), copies used for evaluation purposes (with conditions on how they are used, and for how long) and copies used for distribution purposes. Likewise, there can be 'runtime' versions of some software, which do not require separate paid licences. (It may be difficult to distinguish between runtime and non-runtime versions of such software.)

Backups are problematical legally. Many software contracts only allow for one backup copy for archival purposes, but this is contrary to good IT practice for making backups. However, it is unlikely that a software manufacturer would make an issue of this, or that a court would uphold it if taken that far. The critical issue is that the copies should be purely for backup purposes, with no more copies ever being used (installed or executed) than are licensed. The situation for 'hot' backups is different, because in these cases the backup software is installed. Reference must be made to specific licence terms and conditions in these cases.

A.2 BASIC TYPES OF LICENCE

Licences can have many different characteristics for description purposes. These are described below.

A.2.1 Duration

- **Perpetual** Historically, most licences sold have been perpetual, i.e. the use rights are permanent once purchased
- **Subscription or rental** Licences that can be used for a specific period of time, which can vary from days to years and may or may not include upgrade rights
- **Temporary** In addition to subscription or rental licences, there can be other cases of temporary licences, e.g. pending full payment or receipt of proof of licence.

A.2.2 Measure of usage

- **Per copy: by workstation/seat/device, named user, anonymous user, concurrent user** Historically, most licences sold have been on a per-copy-used basis, with several different units of measure possible. Sometimes multiple users will be allowed per licence (e.g. for some PC-linking software). It should also be noted that licensing is sometimes based on unit counts other than just PCs. For example, printer counts are important in several licensing schemes, e.g. for fonts (where there may be a limit on the number of printers that can download the fonts per licence), and for some networking software node counts. Likewise, mobile devices (PDAs, SmartPhones etc.) have licensing requirements but may not be recognized by many 'traditional' approaches to licence management based just on PCs
- **Concurrent usage** This allows a specified number of users to connect simultaneously to a software application. This is a commonly understood licensing approach, and there are a number of software products to help monitor and control concurrent usage. However, such licences are not as commonly available as previously was the case
- **Per server speed or per processor** These are linked to the speed or power of the server on which they are run, or the number of processors within the server
- **Client/server access** Most licences correspond to physical installations or use of software. However, there is an important category of licences that do not correspond to physical software, and these are frequently misunderstood. These are client access licences, which give a client device the right to access a server package, regardless of whether or not there is client software associated with it. The detailed terms and conditions for such licences prevent software 'tricks' to combine multiple clients into a single channel for licensing purposes
- **Enterprise or site** Increasingly, licences are being sold on an enterprise or site basis that requires just a count of qualifying entities (workstations or employees, most commonly). This is usually easier for administration purposes, especially in organizations with limited SAM capabilities. Nonetheless, people who do not understand the contractual definition of the enterprise may try to apply 'per-copy' counting rules instead. A further complication may be that qualifying workstations or employees/contractors may not be simple to identify
- **Other complexities** Other more complex situations also exist with regard to licensing and the use of techniques such as multiplexing,

clustering, virtualization, shared services, thin client, roaming services, and cloud and grid computing. These situations can be very complex, often expensive and invariably need careful management on an individual case-by-case basis.

A.2.3 Upgrades

There are many different types of upgrade that are sold, each typically with detailed conditions as to what is acceptable as a basis for the upgrade. A common problem is that upgrade licences are purchased, for which there are no qualifying underlying licences, e.g. competitive upgrades may have been purchased without any competitive product actually being owned, in which case the licences are invalid for use.

- Version upgrades normally refer to a later release of the same product
- Product upgrades normally refer to changes within a product family, e.g. a partial suite of products being upgraded to a more extensive suite of the same product family
- Competitive upgrades normally refer to upgrades based on competitive products
- Language upgrades allow the use of a more expensive product with different/additional language capabilities
- Upgrade insurance (maintenance etc.). Many software manufacturers offer upgrade 'insurance' under a variety of names. Essentially, they all allow the purchasers to use any upgrades that are released during the period of the insurance. A problem that occurs sometimes is that organizations forget the upgrade rights they purchased with this insurance because they do not perform the physical upgrade during the same time period. They may then purchase the upgrades again later when the physical upgrade is performed

- Technology guarantees etc. Technology guarantees are limited-duration upgrade rights that a software manufacturer may grant to purchasers of one version of software, when a new version is expected but not yet released. It is important to note these rights when they are issued, as they may be difficult to determine retroactively.

A.2.4 End-user type

- **Commercial vs. academic** There is typically less expensive pricing for academic users than for commercial users. The risk is that academic copies may be purchased in situations that do not qualify
- **Commercial vs. personal** Some licences distinguish between commercial use and personal use, charging for the former but not the latter. This is common, for example, with some shareware/freeware packages.

A.2.5 Licence management responsibility

- **Vendor-managed usage (VMU)** Technical licence management products are in place with some software manufacturers. In these cases, end-users can be largely absolved of the licence management aspect of SAM, although it may still be desirable as a check on the correctness of software manufacturer measurements, and to facilitate strategic planning
- **Customer-managed usage (CMU)** Most licence management requires customer management, and that is the focus of this guide.

A.2.6 Other

- **Suite**   A group of applications sold together. The terms of the licence normally preclude the individual applications being separated and used individually on separate devices, or by different users simultaneously
- **Secondary usage**   A licence that provides for the use of software either by secondary users or in a secondary location. Examples are the ability to use one licence on a desktop and a laptop, or on both a work computer and a home computer. Secondary usage rights may come with the main licence, or may be sold separately
- **Locked licence**   This requires an activation key and is not readily copied or moved
- **Token-activated**   This uses a dongle or security device to restrict usage
- **Serialized licence**   Identifiable by a unique serial number, therefore easier to check authenticity.

A.3   TYPES OF LICENCES BY SALES CHANNEL

Frequently there are differences in licence terms and conditions depending on the sales channel. In particular:

- **Original equipment manufacturers (OEMs)** They often have their own licensing terms for software that they supply together with equipment. One of the most significant conditions typically attached to such software is that the software can only be used on the original equipment. If the equipment is replaced, the software cannot be moved to a new machine (although any upgrades used may be movable). The end-user licence agreement (EULA) for OEM software is normally between the equipment manufacturer and the end-user, and not between the software manufacturer and the end-user
- **Retail**   Software sold in retail packaging is the closest to a typical hardware product in terms of physical characteristics. It is also usually the most expensive, and maintaining the proof of licence is typically the most onerous for this type of product
- **Low volume**   There are low-volume methods of purchasing software licences that do not require the signing of a contract with the software manufacturer, but which usually require user registration. Media may have to be purchased separately. There may be some limited audit rights associated with such licences
- **High volume**   The high-volume methods of purchasing software licences generally require a signed contract with the software manufacturer. There are typically several levels of contract and/or pricing. This type of contract typically gives the software manufacturer significant audit rights
- **Service provider**   Software is increasingly being made available through hosting organizations, or application service providers (ASPs). This is normally on a rental or other temporary rights basis
- **Solution provider**   Software and sometimes hardware from multiple manufacturers may be bundled by a 'solution provider' as a turn-key package. These range from small packages to major enterprise resource planning (ERP) systems. These bundled licences need to be recognized as part of overall software asset management

■ **Shareware, freeware and public domain software**   These tend to be distributed via the internet rather than through commercial resellers. There may be many shareware, freeware and public domain software packages in use within an organization, e.g. zipping utilities. These types of software should be subject to the same controls as software procured from major software manufacturers

- shareware – users are encouraged to copy the program for preview purposes. If the user intends to keep using it then a licence fee must be paid to the developer

- freeware – no licence fee is paid but these programs still come with a licence agreement that could potentially be violated. See also 'Open-source' below

- public domain – this must be clearly marked as such, and means the copyright holder has relinquished all rights to the software so it can be freely copied, modified, enhanced etc.

■ **Open-source**   This is an increasingly common version of freeware that, as a condition of its licence, requires the source code to be provided and to be modifiable. The licences themselves are free, but there may be charges for media and distribution.

A.4   COUNTERFEITS

Counterfeit software is software that falsely appears to be genuine, including its related proof of licence materials. This is not the same as pirated software, as with 'hard-disk loading', whereby a dealer may load unlicensed copies of legitimate software onto the machines they sell. With 'hard-disk loading', there are typically no materials supplied that purport to have come from the software manufacturer.

There is a serious risk of an organization purchasing counterfeit software. This risk is greater than many organizations realize because of the sophistication of counterfeiters, and the lack of attention that may be paid by some resellers and end-user organizations to this issue. The risks of using counterfeit software include:

■ Not being licensed for the software being used

■ Loss of money spent on the counterfeit software (rather than an apparent saving)

■ Being in violation of copyright and trademark legislation through possession of the counterfeit products.

The main factors for increased risk of counterfeit software are:

■ **Status of suppliers and source of product**   For some software manufacturers and some licensing programs, software may be purchased directly from the manufacturers or from authorized resellers. There is no real risk of purchasing counterfeit products directly from the manufacturer, and a significantly reduced risk from an authorized reseller. A reseller with no special status, selling goods that purport to come from the 'grey market', may involve significantly more risk. 'Grey market' products in particular are at high risk of being counterfeit, because this is a common way of a reseller trying to explain the low cost of counterfeit products

■ **Length of distribution chain**   Collateral or proof of licence received directly from a software manufacturer is the best guarantee of authenticity. The more tiers there are in the distribution channel between the software manufacturer and the end-customer, the greater the risk of counterfeit product entering the chain

- **Size of reseller**   Larger resellers usually are more established, and have more to lose if caught selling counterfeit products. They should take extra measures to ensure they are dealing only with genuine products. Smaller resellers may be more susceptible to selling counterfeit software, knowingly or unknowingly
- **Geographical location**   If the transaction is based in a country with less stringent copyright/trademark laws or enforcement, the risk of counterfeit software increases.

These risk factors are for awareness only – they are not absolute. There are resellers who are small, at the end of long distribution chains or based in countries with weak intellectual property protection but selling genuine products. Nevertheless, the buyer has a particular duty of care to ensure that the product they are buying is genuine even though there are increased risk factors.

Definitive guidance about how to identify counterfeits is beyond the scope of this publication. However, the following guidelines are suggested:

- Assess the likelihood of counterfeit product based on the risk factors involved (see above)
- Be knowledgeable about each software manufacturer's security features designed to fight counterfeiting. Descriptions of these may typically be found on software manufacturers' websites
- Make it clear to your resellers in advance that you will check for the authenticity of the product supplied, especially if the price looks particularly low
- Review all software collateral received for relevant security features, with a degree of attention corresponding to the risk factors involved
- Refer to the software manufacturer directly in cases of doubt.

A.5   WHAT IS 'PROOF OF LICENCE'?

'Proof of licence' is what a court will accept as proof of a legal entity having a licence. However, it should rarely be necessary to resort to court. Each software manufacturer in general states the requirements for their proof of licence, so no hard and fast rules can be given here. As a general principle, proof of licence requires some form of evidence directly from the software manufacturer. Evidence of payments made to a reseller, or licence confirmations produced by a reseller, will not usually constitute acceptable proof of licence. The spectrum of types of evidence for having a licence includes the following, of which the first three are usually the most important:

- Printed licence confirmation documents from software manufacturers (with security features)
- Electronic licence confirmation documents from software manufacturers held on controlled-access websites
- Certificates of authenticity that are typically engraved, or with other security features. These may be:
  - loose pieces of paper
  - pieces of paper pasted onto manual covers
  - labels glued onto equipment
  - labels printed or glued on retail boxes.

Although certificates of authenticity are important, backup collateral is often required, because under some circumstances a certificate of authenticity may be attached to an illegal/counterfeit copy, e.g. an unlabelled certificate of authenticity for a less expensive product repackaged with a counterfeit more expensive product.

- Media (CDs, disks, DVDs, plus associated jewel case boxes often with serial numbers, especially for retail products)
- Documentation (especially for older retail products)
- Volume purchasing contracts
- Purchasing records or analyses provided by software manufacturers, including proof of payment
- Free-standing letters or other documentation from software manufacturers confirming a grant of licences
- Invoices from resellers, including proof of payment
- Sales documentation. It may be desirable to keep copies of sales documentation, e.g. product brochures, to clarify the licences that are included with specific packaged products, e.g. OEM products. The descriptions given on invoices in such cases are often insufficient to clarify what licences are included. In the absence of other stronger documentation, this may be important in helping to establish licence ownership.

> **Example of contractual definition of proof of volume licences**
>
> 'This agreement, the applicable enrolment, the enrolled affiliate's order confirmation ... together with proof of payment, will be the enrolled affiliate's evidence of all licences obtained under its enrolment.'

It is important to emphasize that a 'licence confirmation' document produced by a reseller is usually not an acceptable proof of licence, regardless of how impressive it may seem, sometimes with its own security features. Such documents have been produced by many resellers for a number of reasons, such as the delays in customers getting software manufacturer confirmations, and the consolidation of reporting that may occur in software manufacturer confirmations. However, they are not proof of licence, and may create significant legal and financial exposures.

'End-user licence agreement' is another term that is often used in licensing, especially for retail products. The EULA should be retained just as contracts are retained. Its main purpose is to document the terms and conditions of a licence. It is typically provided in soft copy, or in a printed format without any security features. It generally does not provide proof of licence unless it has security features.

The simple rule to follow is to check with the software vendor directly about what they require you to retain. You may well want to renegotiate on this if you feel the administrative tasks would be onerous. Any such 'special dispensations' should be obtained from the vendor in writing.

A.6 PHYSICAL MANAGEMENT OF SOFTWARE LICENCES

A number of challenges are associated with the physical management of licences:

- **Varied physical characteristics** The different types of collateral that can constitute proof of licence have a wide variety of forms and storage characteristics

- **High risk of loss**   There is a high risk of loss of many types of proof of licence, especially in decentralized environments
- **Risk of holding counterfeit licences**   See section A.4
- **Implementing an effective physical management system**   There need to be separate systems for physical storage, and for recording what is in physical storage (similar to the difference between a warehouse, and the stock control records for the warehouse)
- **Linking multiple licences to determine 'effective' licences**   One current 'effective' licence may require many prior purchases. For example, a single effective licence may be the result of a series of upgrades on an earlier product, and the documentation needs to be retained and linked to show how they build on each other. The associated risk is that of double counting of licences, i.e. that all of these documents will be considered individual licences and totalled, rather than considered together as contractually required. There is also a risk of double counting licences when there are multiple forms of support, e.g. certificates of authenticity (COAs) and invoices.

A.6.1 Physical characteristics

Some types of proof of licence are easy to store in traditional filing systems, most notably printed 'volume-licensing confirmations'. However, the majority are more difficult to store. In particular:

- **OEM operating system licences**   Most OEM operating system COAs are now physically fixed to a PC, and cannot be removed without effectively destroying them. There is no option for separate physical storage of this document, and it can be controlled only in a database.

Barcode readers may be used to capture the relevant information
- **Electronic confirmations**   Many software manufacturers' volume licence confirmation documents now are purely electronic. Although the online copy is definitive, it is prudent to print a copy and treat the printout as if it was a hard-copy original licence confirmation, for ease of reference and as backup for the electronic online version
- **Media**   This is primarily an issue for older software, or where current licences are based on upgrades from older licences where media formed part of the proof of licence. As an example, a company may have purchased large quantities of software via a non-volume channel, so that there is a CD to keep with each. There may have been successive upgrades, including to competitive products, but the original CD is still part of the proof of original licence on which all successive upgrades are based
- **Manuals**   This is also primarily an issue for older software, especially for some software where the certificates of authenticity were pasted to manual covers. If the manuals were given to end-users, the certificates were likely to be lost. However, keeping them centrally in manual form was also problematical. One solution practised by some organizations was to rip off and store the covers with their certificates, and throw away the manuals.

If you have a large quantity of bulky support collateral for early licences, such as CDs, it is worth asking the software manufacturer of your latest licences if they will accept in writing as valid a certificate of destruction from a recognized destruction agent, citing relevant details of the materials destroyed. However, there have been situations where software manufacturers have refused to allow the destruction of CDs even though they were very old.

A.6.2 High risk of loss

There is a high risk of loss of physical licences, especially in decentralized environments where the importance of physical proof of licence is not recognized. This is a significant cause of financial loss, when organizations cannot prove the licences that they assume they have purchased and need to repurchase to prove compliance. There is also a heightened risk of loss in centralized environments to a catastrophic event such as a fire. To minimize these risks, a centralized approach is most appropriate, with off-site backup copies of licence inventory records kept against the risk of catastrophic events.

A.6.3 Implementing an effective physical management system

The physical management system for licences may be just a filing cabinet in a very small organization, but for most organizations this will not be sufficient. There should be two separate parts to the system: a storage system for physical documents and other evidence; and an inventory system to record what is there. Again, in small organizations, the inventory may be kept simply in a spreadsheet, but this will typically be inadequate. What is recommended is a document management system that can keep scanned copies of all physical documents. The physical documents can then be filed away securely without any need for normal access, with reliance placed instead on the scanned images.

Some documentation that legally may form part of the proof of licence, should already be covered by other document management systems, e.g. invoices and contracts. Depending on the functionality of the relevant systems, there may be no need to do anything further. Alternatively, it may be preferable for practical reasons to include copies of such documentation in the licensing document management system. For example, it is sometimes difficult for organizations to retrieve back copies of invoices when they are needed several years later, after system changes or archiving.

A.7 OTHER COMMON LICENSING PROBLEMS

Any of the issues discussed in this appendix may represent a problem. However, the following are some common problem areas encountered not already specifically discussed:

- **Software licensing for subcontractors/ agents** It should be clear when contractors are employed, who is responsible for which licences. Typically, the organization will be responsible for any software it installs on the contractor's machines, and for relevant licences etc.
- **Software licensing for partially owned subsidiaries** Volume-licensing agreements may have conditions concerning which entities may purchase licences under the agreements. It is a common problem that these terms may be breached by providing software to affiliates that do not qualify.

Appendix B: Considerations in selecting SAM tools

Appendix B: Considerations in selecting SAM tools

This appendix supports Chapter 7, with which it should be read. The principal objective of using a tool should be to automate a process to make its operation as efficient as possible.

B.1 GENERAL POINTS OF CONSIDERATION

The following is a sample list of best-practice requirements that organizations should consider when evaluating the functional abilities of SAM tools:

- A careful definition and evaluation of tool requirements has been performed before selection (SoR)
- All the mandatory and desirable functional tool requirements are based on a defined ICT process:
  - all mandatory requirements covered
  - the tool provides a minimum of 80% compliance for all operational requirements
  - the tool does not require extensive tailoring or product customization
  - the tool supports the SAM processes and is also conformant with ITIL and ISO/IEC 20000 principles
  - the tool satisfies current and future business requirements
- The tool conforms with overall technology and management architectures, policies and strategies
- The tool provides the required interfaces with systems management tools
- The tool provides the required interfaces with business process such as HR, financial, and research and development.

Some points that organizations should consider when evaluating the functionality of a SAM tool are:

- Data structure, data handling and integration
- Integration of multi-vendor infrastructure components, and the need to absorb new components in the future – these will place particular demands on the data handling and modelling capabilities of the tool
- Conformity to international open standards
- Integration with other existing management tools
- Flexibility in implementation, usage and data sharing
- Usability – the ease of use permitted by the user interface
- Support for monitoring service levels – response and resolution
- Distributed clients with a centralized shared database (e.g. client server)
- Conversion, import and export requirements for previously tracked data
- Data backup, integrity, control and security
- Support options provided by the tool vendor
- Organizational constraints:
  - impact on the organization
  - staff availability, experience and skill sets
- Implementation complexity

■ Role-based access control (for corporate organizations that allow different access levels for different roles and levels)

■ Costs:
  ● software/hardware (purchase and installation)
  ● licences/training/development and customization
  ● consulting.

B.2 PRACTICAL GUIDELINES FOR THE SELECTION OF SAM TOOLS

Consideration must be given to the exact requirements of the tool. What are the mandatory requirements and what are the desired requirements? Some practical guidelines are listed here:

■ A correct balance needs to be struck between defining your organization's own requirements for SAM, and possibly modifying those requirements to fit existing tool capabilities. In theory, tools should be modified if necessary to meet an organization's own requirements. In practice, however, SAM requirements should not be unique so that each organization needs extensive customization to meet them. Therefore, you should still define requirements carefully, and assess existing tools against those requirements. You should have existing tools that meet most of those requirements. If not, then your organization should seriously review its stated requirements to see if they are realistic, rather than immediately going for a custom solution

■ It is essential to have an SoR for use during the selection process This statement can be used as a 'tick list'. The requirements can be rated in

terms of mandatory facilities, needed facilities and 'nice to have' facilities

■ The tool must be adequately flexible to support the required access rights. You must be able to determine who is permitted to access what data and for what purpose, e.g. read access to customers

■ In the early stages consideration must also be given to the platform on which the tool will be expected to operate – this may be on existing hardware and software or a new purchase. There may be restrictions laid down by ICT strategy, for example, all new products may have to reside on specific servers. This would restrict the products that could be included in the evaluation process

■ Make sure that the procurement fits within existing approved budgets

■ There are many SAM tools available. Do not restrict your choice to the one(s) your organization knows about. Surf the web, look at SAM publications, ask other organizations, ask consultants or talk to industry forum(s) to see what products are available. There may be a user group for the product – if there is, talk to the chairperson, as this may lead to useful feedback

■ During the early stages of the vetting process, think about vendor and tool credibility. Are they still going to be supporting the purchase in a few months or a year's time? Consider the past record of the supplier as well as that of the tool. Telephone the supplier service desk to see how easy it is to get through, and ask some test questions to assess technical competence

■ Ask the vendor to arrange a visit to a reference site to see what their experience is with the tool in practice – if possible without the vendor or supplier present. Make sure that your organization has similar requirements of the tool. See the tool in operation and speak to the users about their experiences, both initially and ongoing

- Do not limit your requirements to functionality. Ask about the product's ability to perform, enlarge the size of the databases, recover from failure and maintain data integrity. Does the product conform to international standards? Is it efficient enough to enable you to meet your SLRs?

- Verify the tools chosen for ease of deployment and ensure there are no detrimental effects on the functioning of the system

- Assess the management reports generated by the tool. In some tools, the generation of meaningful reports can be a cumbersome and time-consuming task. To monitor the output of the processes, the tool should have many methods of aggregating the data in meaningful and, for the business, understandable ways

- Assess the training needs of the organization and evaluate the capability of the supplier to provide the appropriate training. In particular, consider training costs, training location, time required and how soon after training the tool will be in use. During the implementation process, ensure that sufficient training is provided – think about how the new tool will impact both ICT and customer

- Ensure that interfaces with other tools and telephony are functioning correctly. It is wise to identify whether the planned combination has been used (or tried) elsewhere, and with what results. Consider trial or parallel running before finally going live

- Verify the project by running a pilot to ensure reporting structures and data capture meet the objectives and requirements of SAM.

A much more detailed evaluation must now be completed. Demonstrations of the products need to be arranged. Ensure that all relevant members of staff are involved. Be wary of demonstrations – always see the live product in operation. If possible, provide the test data and assess the provided results against expectations. Be cautious of being promised things in the next release. Use a reference site to confirm impressions from the demonstration. Use the SoR and adjust the 'tick list' during the demonstrations of the products. Refer to this later to assist in reducing the shortlist to the final chosen product.

The work obviously does not end when the product has been selected. In many ways, this could be considered as only the beginning. The tool now has to be implemented. Once the hardware platform has been prepared, and the software loaded, data population needs to be considered. What, where from, how and when? Timing is important to the implementation, testing and finally going live processes. Resources must be available to ensure success. In other words, do not schedule during a known busy period, such as year-end processing.

Following live implementation, hold regular meetings with both ICT and customers to ensure the agreed benefits have been realized. Some aspects may have to be refined. During this process, also consider the performance of the supplier. If they have not performed to your expectations, they should be managed and advised (in writing) as soon as possible.

Appendix C: Possible
SAM database contents

C

Appendix C: Possible SAM database contents

This appendix gives suggestions for the possible physical storage contents and corresponding electronic databases for SAM. See Figure 7.1 in Chapter 7 for how these relate to SAM overall, and to the ITIL concepts of the definitive media library and the CMS.

C.1 SOFTWARE LICENCE INVENTORY

Table C.1 Licence information and inventory

Field type	Comments
CMS configuration item (CI) attributes	These are the types of attributes for identification of a CI within the CMS, additional to the detailed fields below:
	■ CI name
	■ Copy or serial number
	■ Category (e.g. software, documentation, media)
	■ Type (amplifying information to category, e.g. program module)
	■ Owner responsible
	■ Responsibility date (that the owner became responsible)
	■ Accepted date (satisfactorily tested)
	■ Parent CI relationships (not already included below)
	■ Child CI relationships (not already included below)
	■ Other CI relationships (not already included below)
	■ Request for change (RFC) numbers affecting this CI
	■ Change records affecting this CI
	■ Problem records affecting this CI
	■ Incident records affecting this CI

Table C.1 Licence information and inventory – *continued*

Summary control information	
Licence status and counts	Licence status and use counts for each status (especially for volume licences). Status can be: ■ Current effective licence – used ■ Current effective licence – unused ■ Subsumed licence (e.g. a later upgrade licence is based on it) ■ Disposed licence (e.g. transferred in part to demerged units)
Where used	Link(s) to where the licence is used. This depends on the type of licensing, but could be: ■ Specific PC ■ Specific server and/or processor ■ Named person ■ Named site
Exception flags	Multiple flags possible, for example: ■ Underlying licence not identified for upgrade licence ■ Full proof of licence not yet located ■ Licence not yet reported – periodic reporting required
Cost	Original cost, current depreciated cost plus currency name
Cost centre	Currently assigned cost centre
Basic reference information	
Licence number	Unique licence reference number, e.g. from the software manufacturer licence confirmation document (as opposed to the reseller confirmation document)
Reseller confirmation document	Unique confirmation document reference number as provided by a reseller
Ordered product	Description of product
Ordered version	
Ordered quantity	
Software manufacturer	
Software manufacturer part number	

Table C.1 Licence information and inventory – *continued*

Platform	Hardware or specific operating system under which the software runs
Licensor	Normally the software manufacturer, but could be the OEM, a system integrator etc.
Licensing programme	For example, retail, OEM, various volume-licensing programmes
Volume-licensing programme reference	Contract reference if obtained through a volume-licensing programme
Purchase order (PO) number	
PO date	
Reseller	
Reseller part number	Is often different from software manufacturer part number, and may be needed to reconcile to reseller invoices and reports
Invoice number	
Invoice date	
Country of usage reported	Country in which the software will be used, as required for some software manufacturer volume reporting
Ordering location as shown by software manufacturer	Ordering location or entity as recorded by software manufacturer, for the purpose of reconciling internal records to software manufacturer confirmations and records
Ordering location as shown by reseller	Ordering location or entity as recorded by reseller, for the purpose of reconciling internal records to reseller reports and records
Proof of licence	Cross-reference(s) to specific documentation that provides proof of licence, and where it is physically located
Media	Cross-reference(s) to media provided with licence, if relevant
Documentation	Cross-reference(s) to documentation provided with licence, if relevant
Product components	For products that consist of a suite of other products, a list of those components to facilitate identification and linking
Current entitlement of original licence purchased	
Product	

Table C.1 Licence information and inventory – *continued*

Version	
Basis for enhanced entitlement and cross-reference	The specified licence may have a different product entitlement from the name given on the initial order. Possible reasons include: ■ Upgrade insurance ■ Technology guarantees ■ Other software manufacturer announcements
Terms and conditions	
Source references	Cross-reference(s) to specific documentation of licensing terms and conditions
Licensing basis	For example, per PC, per device, per user, total number of users (concurrent use), per mailbox, per five printers, per location, per subsidiary, per organization
Expiry date	Not applicable for permanent licences, valid date, e.g. for upgrade insurance or for rental licences
Product substitution rights	For example, downgrade rights, language version substitution rights
Secondary rights	For example, home-use rights, joint desktop and laptop rights
Transferability	For example: ■ Freely transferable (e.g. retail products) ■ Transferable only together with hardware (e.g. most OEM products) ■ Individual counts transferable only within purchasing entity, entire licence freely transferable (e.g. some low-end volume licences) ■ Individual counts transferable within affiliate companies, external transfers subject to restrictions (e.g. some high-end volume licences)
External licence transfer requirements	For example: ■ Formal documentation required? ■ Software manufacturer notification required?

Table C.1 Licence information and inventory – *continued*

Linkages:

■ Upgrades from	Linkages to the underlying licences which this licence is upgrading
■ Upgrades to	Linkages to the subsequent licences which upgrade this licence
■ Secondary use	Linkages between licences if separate licences are required for primary and secondary use, e.g. for home use

Upgrade insurance details (where applicable)

Period	Beginning and end dates during which insurance is applicable
Notice date(s)	Dates when notice must be given to extend, or to cancel automatic renewal

C.2 INSTALLED SOFTWARE INVENTORY

Table C.2 Inventory of installed software

Field type	*Comments*
CMS configuration item attributes	See previous section for explanation
Summary control information	
Installation status	For example, full/partial
Licence used	Link to licence to cover this usage, or not applicable if no licence required (e.g. internally developed applications)
Exception flags	Multiple flags possible, for example: ■ Apparently unlicensed installation ■ Apparently incomplete de-installation
Basic reference information	
Product	
Version	
Updates installed	Updates for the current version of the software, not new versions

Table C.2 Inventory of installed software – *continued*

Security patches installed	
Hardware on which installed	
Country of usage	Country in which software is actually being used, as required for some software manufacturer reporting. May also be important to help track licence compliance on a country-by-country basis for dealing with local authorities
Cost centre of hardware owner	
Date of last discovery	
Metrics	Metrics used for identifying software
Date first discovered	

C.3   SOURCE DOCUMENTATION

The following types of physical documentation will generally need to be filed. It is recommended that copies be scanned and filed in an electronic document management system, if possible, to ensure better availability of the information as well as greater security for the source documents. An indexing system will be needed to allow cross-referencing from different databases.

Some documentation is now available electronically (e.g. some software manufacturer licence confirmations, terms and conditions documents, general licensing information). These electronic documents generally should be included in the same filing system as similar types of physical documents.

Table C.3 Filing of source documentation

Documentation type	Examples
Contracts	Contracts plus amendments – with software manufacturers (master agreements etc.), resellers, outsourcers
SLAs	With internal units and with outsourcers
Terms and conditions	Various formats. Volume-licensing versions may be updated periodically and downloaded electronically
Proof of licence documentation	Licence confirmations, copies of invoices and any other documentation required not already included in the filing system. See Chapter 5 and Appendix A for further discussion
Price lists	
Copies of other relevant internal transaction documentation, if not readily available from alternative systems	Examples are: ■ Copies of internal orders placed ■ Copies of work/installation orders ■ Copies of purchase orders placed
Purchase record downloads	From software manufacturers, resellers.
Correspondence	With resellers, software manufacturers etc.
Licensing programme descriptions	From software manufacturers
Licensing explanations	From software manufacturers

C.4 WORKING DOCUMENTATION

It will generally be desirable to file the following types of physical working documentation formally. (Some of this will be in electronic format.)

Table C.4 Filing of working documentation

Documentation type	Examples
Compliance process documentation	Documentation of the results of compliance processes as described in section 5.4. These include: ■ Periodic licence compliance reconciliations ■ Verification and audit checks (and problem analysis of cause of discrepancies) ■ Security compliance (e.g. completeness and timeliness of security patch installation, and problem analysis of cause of discrepancies) ■ Other policy and procedure compliance
Process improvement reviews	

C.5 MEDIA

There needs to be inventory control over physical media as well as over distribution copies of software which often may be located on servers. Some specific organizational approaches are recommended by software manufacturers for their own volume-licensing media.

C.6 GUIDANCE DOCUMENTATION

It will generally be desirable to file copies of SAM guidance documentation from all sources, including software manufacturers, resellers and professional sources (such as for this guide).

C.7 HARDWARE INVENTORY

It is not in the scope of this guide to cover hardware except for those aspects that are necessary for effective SAM. One of these aspects is the identification of hardware characteristics that affect software licensing. It may be desirable to include flags in hardware inventories to facilitate software licensing calculations. For example:

■ If a PC is a qualifying PC for the purposes of site licensing counts

■ Processing power for licensing, which is calculated on this basis

■ Who owns the machine and is responsible for licensing (in the case of hosting service providers and similar).

Appendix D: Choosing a SAM partner

Appendix D: Choosing a SAM partner

Table D.1 below identifies some criteria worth investigating when selecting a SAM partner. The focus of this appendix is on choosing a SAM consultant, but much of it can be applied to other types of SAM partner. (See Chapter 8 for a more general discussion of the types of SAM partner and the services they provide).

At present, there is limited depth in the software asset management market. Nonetheless, just about every organization working in any related area will claim to be able to offer SAM consultancy and related services. As the need for SAM emerges, it is anticipated that yet more companies will enter the SAM provider market.

The most critical selection criterion in most cases will probably be the skills and experience of the individuals who will be responsible for the services to be provided, more so than the overall experience of the organization for which they work, although both are important.

There is probably no perfect partner, and it may be appropriate to have more than one partner working together. At least one partner should probably have extensive and practical current licensing knowledge, such as a good reseller should have.

Table D.1 Importance criteria for potential SAM partners

Key to importance weighting – low (L), medium (M), high (H)

Reference	Criteria	Importance	Comments
Qualifications and capabilities of the organization			
1	Can the organization demonstrate experience for the type of assistance sought?	H	
2	Does the organization have established methodologies and tools for the type of assistance sought?	H	
3	How long has the organization been providing the type of assistance sought?	M	
4	What quality of licensing expertise is expected to be applied as part of the service to be provided? Examine details of people, training and qualifications, and length of time in jobs	H	This is generally one of the most important issues in the selection of a potential partner. The expertise needs to be realistically available, and applied to the work without having to make exceptional requests

Table D.1 Importance criteria for potential SAM partners – _continued_

Reference	Criteria	Importance	Comments
5	If the service requires determination of effective licensing, what relevant tools and methodologies can be demonstrated?	H	One of the most complex issues in licence compliance is the determination of current effective licences taking into account: all past licence purchases including full and upgrade products of various types; upgrade insurance and its timing relative to release dates of new versions; and detailed contractual issues about how previous licences relate to site licences (i.e. are they subsumed by the new licences, or are they separate and available for redeployment)
6	Does the organization offer other related services that may complement the type of assistance currently sought?	L	May create synergies, but also may create conflicts of interest – see below
7	Where is the service available geographically?	L	More important for multinational organizations
8	In what languages is the service available?	L	More important for multinational organizations
9	How old is the organization?	L	
10	How financially strong is the organization?	M	More important for organizations where there may need to be a long-term relationship, e.g. with tool vendors or outsourcers
SAM focus			
11	How many people does the organization have, globally and locally, dedicated 100% to providing SAM-type services (not full-time equivalents of people doing other work as well)?	M	This is a good indicator of the seriousness of an organization about SAM
12	Are SAM services provided by a dedicated unit or out of a more generalist unit?	M	This is a good indicator of the seriousness of an organization about SAM

Table D.1 Importance criteria for potential SAM partners – *continued*

Reference	Criteria	Importance	Comments
Conflicts of interest			
13	Is the organization primarily dependent on a particular manufacturer for most of its work?	M	A close relationship with a particular software manufacturer can be an advantage in terms of detailed knowledge of that software manufacturer's products, but needs to be assessed against the possible conflicts of interest involved, e.g. advocating that software manufacturer's products inappropriately, or leaking confidential information back to that software manufacturer
14	Does the organization have vested interests in other areas that might affect the independence of its SAM services, e.g. selling licences, selling and/or installing SAM tools or providing outsourcing services?	M	Involvement in any of these areas can be an advantage because of the additional knowledge it gives to the organization, but needs to be assessed against the possible conflicts of interest involved
15	Does the organization offer its services on a fee basis rather than related to the sale of other products?	M	Fee-based services are generally preferable from an independence point of view
16	Does it appear that the service is being offered as a 'loss-leader' with the objective of cross-selling other services in the future, e.g. as a result of knowing more about internal ICT plans?	H	Loss-leaders may represent false savings. The provider will typically not be able to justify the quality-in-depth that the job requires, and the work may be biased to ensure the creation of new revenue opportunities
Qualifications and capabilities of the principal individuals proposed			
17	Does the individual have demonstrated experience for the type of assistance sought? Over what period?	H	Very important
18	Can the individual answer relevant detailed questions without research during initial discussions?	H	Proof of capabilities
19	Does the individual have qualifications for the type of assistance sought? For example, licensing certifications from software manufacturers	M	

Table D.1 Importance criteria for potential SAM partners – *continued*

Reference	Criteria	Importance	Comments
References			
20	Can you talk privately to at least two references for whom the organization has previously provided similar services, and get good feedback?	H	Very important
Other questions			
21	How well does the organization control its own software assets? Ask to see a live demonstration and talk to end-users	M	Demonstrates how serious the organization is about SAM
22	Does the organization have any other general certifications or qualifications, e.g. ISO certification or software manufacturer certifications?	L	The question is how relevant the certifications are to the services being requested

Appendix E:
The detailed contents of
a SAM business case

Appendix E: The detailed contents of a SAM business case

A business case for the implementation of SAM should contain, where appropriate:

- Identification and quantification of all of the benefits to the business and its customers
- The overall scope, size of the task, objectives, deliverables, impacts, CSFs, KPIs, and business benefits of the proposed solution
- The business sponsor/owner and the stakeholders
- A description of the current situation, including strengths, weaknesses, opportunities and threats
- The strategic fit and details of how the preferred solution conforms to, supports or deviates from existing corporate, business and ICT initiatives, policies, strategies and plans
- Details of how these key strategic objectives and benefits will be achieved
- The implications, risks and impacts of not proceeding with the business case (do nothing)
- A description of the proposed new processes and their objectives
- Details of all constraints and dependencies
- The level of authorization or approval necessary and the required timescale for approval
- Industry considerations:
  - external opportunities and threats
  - market share and competitors
  - present and forecasted volumes
  - regulatory and legislative constraints
  - trends in pricing, quality, standards and technology
  - competitive services and products, their quality and performance
- Details of how the objectives, deliverables, CSFs and business benefits will be monitored and measured, including operational targets
- Details of the project management methods and approach
- Identification and quantification of all risks:
  - description
  - probability
  - impact and analysis of the risk
  - steps taken to manage and minimize the risk
  - any necessary mitigating countermeasures and expenditure
- The preferred solution with its advantages, disadvantages, benefits, risks, costs, resources and timescales, including ongoing requirements and costs
- Alternative solutions considered and their advantages, disadvantages, benefits, risks, costs and timescales, including ongoing requirements and costs, including the 'do nothing' option
- The reasons for selecting any preferred suppliers and rejecting alternative suppliers
- Details of key milestones in the implementation process and overall dependencies
- Details of parent programmes or projects and their interfaces and approval status

- Details of any dependent programmes or projects and their dependencies and approval status
- The authorizing, owning or sponsoring body and budget(s) to be used
- Details of the approach to be adopted (e.g. in-house resources, contracted-in resources or managed service)
- Procurement plans and policies with details of preferred suppliers and their costs and comparative alternatives and their costs
- Financial analysis:
  - financial assumptions
  - initial and ongoing costs
  - financial constraints and budgets
  - payback period and ROI
  - tolerances and sensitivities
  - funding and stakeholders
  - the possible effects on the organization's financial performance and profitability
- Requirements for external resources and finances from other departments and organizations
- Contractual, legal and regulatory issues
- Environmental issues
- Clear, concise and unambiguous summary and recommendations.

Appendix F:
Example contents of a
software policy

F

Appendix F: Example contents of a software policy

An organizational software policy should address:

- Use and misuse of ICT systems including hardware and software
- Software use, licensing and copyright policy
- Use of personal software
- Use of shareware and freeware
- Use of illegal or pirated software
- Requesting and procurement of software, including the business justification and the registration of requests for new or enhanced software
- Software procurement approval process
- Defined ownership, roles and responsibilities for enforcement, administration and non-compliance
- Use of SAM processes and procedures
- Downloading of software
- Use of the internet and email systems
- Copying of software
- Software selection and evaluation process
- Selection of software resellers, suppliers and manufacturers, including a preferred list of suppliers
- A common software distribution and upgrade process
- Protection of the organization's own intellectual property
- Sign-off and acceptance of the software policy by all personnel including all new employees and all contractors
- Responsibilities (by role, not individual) for ownership and monitoring of processes and data
- Methods of disseminating the software policy and any amendments.

The remainder of this appendix contains an example policy document that could be used to develop an organization's hardware and software policy.

F.1 SAMPLE POLICY ON THE USE OF HARDWARE AND SOFTWARE

All ICT resources, including all hardware, software and network systems, provided by the company are to be used only for company business. Use of the company's ICT resources implies that you:

- Assume responsibility for their appropriate use
- Agree to abide by this policy
- Agree to abide by all national and local laws and regulations
- Agree to abide by all software contractual terms and conditions.

All software and hardware purchased for or developed by company employees or persons acting on their behalf will remain the intellectual property of the company and must be used in compliance with all company policies, relevant licences and contractual terms and conditions.

No equipment from outside the company should be used within company premises or connected to the company network without the prior written consent of the information systems (IS) department.

All employees are responsible for reading and complying with all conditions applying to the proper use of company hardware and software.

All software and hardware will be purchased through the IS department to ensure that cost-effective and efficient systems are purchased to corporate standards. All requests for software or hardware should be submitted to IS on the company standard IS request form.

The standard company configurations are documented on the company intranet at

....

These configurations will be fully supported by the IS department. Employees needing configurations or components other than these should submit a standard request with the accompanying justification.

Any violation or contravention of this policy will result in specific action being initiated against the instigator. This will consist of:

■ Disciplinary action as stated within the company's employee handbook
■ Civil or criminal proceedings where appropriate.

F.2 ACKNOWLEDGEMENT OF HARDWARE/SOFTWARE POLICY

This form is used to acknowledge receipt and understanding of and compliance with the company's policy on the use of IS hardware and software. The form should be completed using the following steps:

■ Read and study the company policy on the use of hardware and software
■ Complete and sign the form and return it to IS administration.

I have read a copy of the company policy on the use of hardware and software and I understand and agree to the following:

■ The terms and conditions contained within the policy document
■ That any hardware and software components provided by the company for my use will remain the property of the company
■ That I will make reasonable efforts to protect all components and information provided by the company from theft, damage or corruption
■ That I will not add, modify, change or upgrade any of the software or hardware components provided by the company for my use without the prior written permission of the IS department
■ That I will not copy or duplicate any of the software components provided, or allow any of the components provided to be copied by anyone else
■ That if I leave the company all computer materials, including all hardware, software and information received from the company will be returned prior to my departure
■ That no software will be purchased or downloaded from the internet and installed on any of the equipment received from the company without the prior written permission of the IS department.

Employee name:
Employee title:
Department:
Post:
Location:
Employee signature:
Date:

Further information

Further information

ASSOCIATED REFERENCE BOOKS AND DOCUMENTS

From the Office of Government Commerce

Note: all five titles below are available from www.tso.co.uk

Service Strategy (TSO, 2007). ISBN 9-780113-310456

Service Design (TSO, 2007). ISBN 9-780113-310470

Service Transition (TSO, 2007).
ISBN 9-780113-310487

Service Operation (TSO, 2007).
ISBN 9-780113-310463

Continual Service Improvement (TSO, 2007).
ISBN 9-780113-310494

APPROPRIATE GUIDELINES AND STANDARDS

ISO/IEC 19770–1:2006 Information Technology – Software Asset Management (Part 1: Processes)

ISO/IEC 20000–1:2002 IT Service Management (Part 1: Specification for Service Management)

ISO/IEC 20000–2:2003 IT Service Management (Part 2: Code of Practice for IT Service Management)

PD 0005:2003, IT Service Management:
A Manager's Guide

PD 0015:2002, IT Service Management –
Self Assessment Workbook

BSI website: www.bsi.org.uk

COBIT Executive Summary (version 4.1)

COBIT Framework, Control Objectives, Management Guidelines, Maturity Models (version 4.1)

ISACA website: http://www.isaca.org/cobit.htm

Abbreviations
and glossary

Abbreviations

ASP	application service provider
BRM	business relationship management
BSI	British Standards Institute
BSA	Business Software Alliance
CAL	client access licence
CBA	cost–benefit analysis
CI	configuration item
CMDB	configuration management database
CMS	configuration management system
CMU	customer-managed usage
COA	certificate of authenticity
COBIT	Control OBjectives for Information and related Technology
CSF	critical success factor
DML	definitive media library
EULA	end-user licence agreement
FAST	Federation Against Software Theft
ICT	information and communications technologies
IS	information systems
ISO	International Organization for Standardization
ITAM	IT asset management
ITIL	Information technology infrastructure library
ITSCM	IT service continuity management
itSMF	IT Service Management Forum
KPI	key performance indicator
NAO	National Audit Office
OEM	original equipment manufacturer
OGC	Office of Government Commerce
OLA	operational level agreement
PDA	personal digital assistant
ROI	return on investment
SACM	service asset and configuration management
SAM	software asset management
SIIA	Software and Information Industry Association
SKMS	service knowledge management system
SLA	service level agreement
SLM	service level management
SLR	service level requirement
SoR	statement of requirements
SPA	Software Publishers Association
TCO	total cost of ownership
ToR	terms of reference
VMU	vendor-managed usage

Glossary

alert

A warning that a threshold has been reached, something has changed, or a failure has occurred. Alerts are often created and managed by system management tools and are managed by the event management process.

asset

Any resource or capability. Assets of a service provider include anything that could contribute to the delivery of a service. Assets can be one of the following types: management, organization, process, knowledge, people, information, applications, infrastructure, and financial capital.

asset management

Asset management is the process responsible for tracking and reporting the value and ownership of financial assets throughout their lifecycle. Asset management is part of an overall service asset and configuration management process.

availability

Ability of a configuration item or IT service to perform its agreed function when required. Availability is determined by reliability, maintainability, serviceability, performance and security. Availability is usually calculated as a percentage. This calculation is often based on agreed service time and downtime. It is best practice to calculate availability using measurements of the business output of the IT service.

availability management

The process responsible for defining, analysing, planning, measuring and improving all aspects of the availability of IT services. Availability management is responsible for ensuring that all IT infrastructure, processes, tools, roles etc. are appropriate for the agreed service level targets for availability.

balanced scorecard

A management tool developed by Drs Robert Kaplan (Harvard Business School) and David Norton. A balanced scorecard enables a strategy to be broken down into key performance indicators (KPIs). Performance against the KPIs is used to demonstrate how well the strategy is being achieved. A balanced scorecard has four major areas, each of which has a small number of KPIs. The same four areas are considered at different levels of detail throughout the organization.

baseline

A benchmark that is used as a reference point. For example:

- An IT service management baseline can be used as a starting point to measure the effect of a service improvement plan
- A performance baseline can be used to measure changes in performance over the lifetime of an IT service
- A configuration management baseline can be used to enable the IT infrastructure to be restored to a known configuration if a change or release fails.

baseline security

The security level adopted by the ICT organization for its own security and from the point of view of good 'due diligence'.

budgeting

The activity of predicting and controlling the spending of money. Consists of a periodic negotiation cycle to set future budgets (usually annual) and the day-to-day monitoring and adjusting of current budgets.

build

The activity of assembling a number of configuration items to create part of an IT service. The term build is also used to refer to a release that is authorized for distribution, e.g. server build or laptop build.

business case

Justification for a significant item of expenditure. Includes information about costs, benefits, options, issues, risks and possible problems.

business function

A business unit within an organization, e.g. a department, division, branch.

business process

A process that is owned and carried out by the business. A business process contributes to the delivery of a product or service to a business customer, e.g. a retailer may have a purchasing process which helps to deliver services to their business customers. Many business processes rely on IT services.

business recovery plans

Documents describing the roles, responsibilities and actions necessary to resume business processes following a business disruption.

business unit

A segment of the business which has its own plans, metrics, income and costs. Each business unit owns assets and uses these to create value for customers in the form of goods and services.

capacity management

The process responsible for ensuring that the capacity of IT services and the IT infrastructure is able to deliver agreed service level targets in a cost-effective and timely manner. Capacity management considers all resources required to deliver the IT service, and plans for short-, medium- and long-term business requirements.

category

A named group of things that have something in common. Categories are used to group similar things together, e.g. cost types are used to group similar types of cost. Incident categories are used to group similar types of incident, CI types are used to group similar types of configuration item.

change

The addition, modification or removal of anything that could have an effect on IT services. The scope should include all IT services, configuration items, processes, documentation etc.

change control

The procedure to ensure that all changes are controlled, including the submission, analysis, decision-making, approval, implementation and post-implementation of the change.

change history

Information about all changes made to a configuration item during its life. Change history consists of all those change records that apply to the CI.

change log

A log of requests for change raised during the project, showing information on each change, its evaluation, what decisions have been made and its current status, e.g. raised, reviewed, approved, implemented, closed.

change management

The process responsible for controlling the lifecycle of all changes. The primary objective of change management is to enable beneficial changes to be made, with minimum disruption to IT services.

change record

A record containing the details of a change. Each change record documents the lifecycle of a single change. A change record is created for every request for change that is received, even those that are subsequently rejected.

Change records should reference the configuration items that are affected by the change. Change records are stored in the configuration management system.

charging

Requiring payment for IT services. Charging for IT services is optional, and many organizations choose to treat their IT service provider as a cost centre.

classification

The act of assigning a category to something. Classification is used to ensure consistent management and reporting. Configuration items, incidents, problems, changes etc. are usually classified.

client access licence

A licence that permits a client (e.g. a workstation) to access software services on a server. Often there will not be any special software on the client PCs, so the use of this type of licence cannot be measured by counting the installed copies of software. The number of licences required may be determined in different ways depending on the software manufacturer's terms and conditions, e.g. it may be necessary to count client PCs, or to count the number of total users.

COBIT

Control OBjectives for Information and related Technology (COBIT) provides guidance and best practice for the management of IT processes. COBIT is published by the IT Governance Institute. See www.isaca.org/ for more information.

compliance

Ensuring that a standard or set of guidelines is followed, or that proper, consistent accounting or other practices are being employed.

configuration baseline

A baseline of a configuration that has been formally agreed and is managed through the change management process. A configuration baseline is used as a basis for future builds, releases and changes. *See also* baseline.

configuration control

The activity responsible for ensuring that adding, modifying or removing a CI is properly managed, for example by submitting a request for change or service request.

configuration documentation

Documents that define requirements, system design, build, production, and verification for a configuration item.

configuration identification

The activity responsible for collecting information about configuration items and their relationships, and loading this information into the CMDB. Configuration identification is also responsible for labelling the CIs themselves, so that the corresponding configuration records can be found.

configuration item

Any component that needs to be managed in order to deliver an IT service. Information about each configuration item (CI) is recorded in a configuration record within the configuration management system and is maintained throughout its lifecycle by configuration management. CIs are under the control of change management and typically include IT services, hardware, software, buildings, people and formal documentation such as process documentation and service level agreements.

configuration management

The process responsible for maintaining information about configuration items (CIs) required to deliver an IT service, including their relationships. This information is managed throughout the lifecycle of the CI. Configuration management is part of an overall service asset and configuration management process.

configuration management database

A database used to store configuration records throughout their lifecycle. The configuration management system maintains one or more configuration management databases (CMDBs), and each CMDB stores attributes of configuration items (CIs) and their relationships with other CIs.

configuration management system

A set of tools and databases that are used to manage an IT service provider's configuration data. The configuration management system (CMS) also includes information about incidents, problems, known errors, changes and releases, and may contain data about employees, suppliers, locations, business units, customers and users. The CMS includes tools for collecting, storing, managing, updating and presenting data about all configuration items and their relationships. The CMS is maintained by configuration management and is used by all IT service management processes. *See also* configuration management database; service knowledge management system.

configuration structure

The hierarchy and other relationships between all the configuration items that comprise a configuration.

continual service improvement programme

A stage in the lifecycle of an IT service and the title of one of the core ITIL publications. Continual service improvement is responsible for managing improvements to IT service management processes and IT services. The performance of the IT service provider is continually measured and improvements are made to processes, IT services and IT infrastructure in order to increase efficiency, effectiveness and cost-effectiveness.

cost

The amount of money spent on a specific activity, IT service or business unit. Costs consist of real cost (money), notional cost such as people's time and depreciation.

cost–benefit analysis

An activity that analyses and compares the costs and the benefits involved in one or more alternative courses of action. *See also* business case; return on investment.

cost-effectiveness

A measure of the balance between the effectiveness and cost of a service, process or activity. A cost-effective process is one which achieves its objectives at minimum cost.

countermeasure

Can be used to refer to any type of control. The term countermeasure is most often used when referring to measures that increase resilience, fault tolerance or reliability of an IT service.

critical success factor

Something that must happen if a process, project, plan, or IT service is to succeed. Key performance indicators (KPIs) are used to measure the achievement of each critical success factor (CSF). For example a CSF of 'protect IT services when making changes' could be measured by KPIs such as 'percentage reduction of unsuccessful changes', 'percentage reduction in changes causing incidents' etc.

culture

A set of values that is shared by a group of people, including expectations about how people should behave, ideas, beliefs and practices.

customer

Someone who buys goods or services. The customer of an IT service provider is the person or group who defines and agrees the service level targets. The term customers is also sometimes informally used to mean users, for example 'this is a customer-focused organization'.

customer-managed usage

The concept of customers managing their own use of licences, as opposed to the concept of vendor-managed usage (VMU). The focus of this guide is CMU.

definitive media library

One or more locations in which the definitive and approved versions of all software configuration items (CIs) are securely stored. The definitive media library (DML) may also contain associated CIs such as licences and documentation. The DML is a single logical storage area even if there are multiple locations. All software in the DML is under the control of change and release management and is recorded in the configuration management system. Only software from the DML is acceptable for use in a release.

dependency

The direct or indirect reliance of one process or activity on another.

depreciation

A measure of the reduction in value of an asset over its life. This is based on wearing out, consumption or other reduction in the useful economic value.

end-user

See user.

environment

A subset of the IT infrastructure that is used for a particular purpose, for example: live environment, test environment, build environment. It is possible for multiple environments to share a configuration item, for example test and live environments may use different partitions on a single mainframe computer. Also used in the term physical environment to mean the accommodation, air conditioning, power system etc. Environment is also used as a generic term to mean the external conditions that influence or affect something.

financial management

The function and processes responsible for managing an IT service provider's budgeting, accounting and charging requirements.

impact

A measure of the effect of an incident, problem or change on business processes. Impact is often based on how service levels will be affected. Impact and urgency are used to assign priority.

incident

An unplanned interruption to an IT service or a reduction in the quality of an IT service. Failure of a configuration item that has not yet impacted service is also an incident, e.g. failure of one disk from a mirror set.

incident management

The process responsible for managing the lifecycle of all incidents. The primary objective of incident management is to return the IT service to users as quickly as possible.

information and communications technologies

The convergence of information technology, telecommunications and data networking technologies into a single technology.

information security management

The process that ensures the confidentiality, integrity and availability of an organization's assets, information, data and IT services. Information security management usually forms part of an organizational approach to security management which has a wider scope than the IT service provider, and includes handling of paper, building access, phone calls etc., for the entire organization.

International Organization for Standardization

The International Organization for Standardization (ISO) is the world's largest developer of standards. ISO is a non-governmental organization and is a network of the national standards institutes of 156 countries. Further information about ISO is available from www.iso.org.

ISO/IEC 9001

A generic term that refers to a number of international standards and guidelines for quality management systems.

ISO/IEC 19770

ISO standard on software asset management.

ISO/IEC 20000

A generic term that refers to a number of international standards and guidelines for service management.

ISO/IEC 27000

A generic term that refers to a number of international standards and guidelines for information security management.

IT directorate

Senior management within a service provider, charged with developing and delivering IT services. Most commonly used in UK government departments.

IT infrastructure

All of the hardware, software, networks, facilities etc. that are required to develop, test, deliver, monitor, control or support IT services. The term IT infrastructure includes all of the information technology but not the associated people, processes and documentation.

IT service continuity management

The process responsible for managing risks that could seriously impact IT services. ITSCM ensures that the IT service provider can always provide minimum agreed service levels, by reducing the risk to an acceptable level and planning for the recovery of IT services. ITSCM should be designed to support business continuity management.

IT infrastructure library

A set of best-practice guidance for IT service management. ITIL is owned by the Office of Government Commerce and consists of a series of publications giving guidance on the provision of quality IT services, and on the processes and facilities needed to support them. See www.itil.co.uk for more information.

key performance indicator

A metric that is used to help manage a process, IT service or activity. Many metrics may be measured, but only the most important of these are defined as key performance indicators (KPIs) and used to actively manage and report on the process, IT service or activity. KPIs should be selected to ensure that efficiency, effectiveness and cost-effectiveness are all managed. *See* critical success factor.

known error

A problem that has a documented root cause and a workaround. Known errors are created and managed throughout their lifecycle by problem management. Known errors may also be identified by development or suppliers.

lifecycle

The various stages in the life of an IT service, configuration item, incident, problem, change etc. The lifecycle defines the categories for status and the status transitions that are permitted. For example:

- The lifecycle of an application includes requirements, design, build, deploy, operate, optimize
- The expanded incident lifecycle includes detect, respond, diagnose, repair, recover, restore
- The lifecycle of a server may include: ordered, received, in test, live, disposed etc.

metric

Something that is measured and reported to help manage a process, IT service or activity.

novation

The formal process of substituting legal obligations, e.g. changing one party to a contract for another when the original party has gone out of legal existence to be replaced by a new one.

operational cost

Cost resulting from running the IT services. Often repeating payments, e.g. staff costs, hardware maintenance and electricity (also known as 'current expenditure' or 'revenue expenditure').

operational level agreement

An agreement between an IT service provider and another part of the same organization. An operational level agreement (OLA) supports the IT service provider's delivery of IT services to customers. The OLA defines the goods or services to be provided and the responsibilities of both parties. For example, there could be an OLA:

- Between the IT service provider and a procurement department to obtain hardware in agreed times.
- Between the service desk and a support group to provide incident resolution in agreed times.

operation

Day-to-day management of an IT service, system, or other configuration item. Operation is also used to mean any pre-defined activity or transaction, e.g. loading a magnetic tape, accepting money at a point of sale, or reading data from a disk drive.

organization

A company, legal entity or other institution. Examples of organizations that are not companies include the International Organization for Standardization or itSMF (IT Service Management Forum). The term organization is sometimes used to refer to any entity which has people, resources and budgets, e.g. a project or business unit.

organizational culture

The whole of the ideas, corporate values, beliefs, practices, expectations about behaviour and daily customs that are shared by the employees in an organization.

outsourcing

Using an external service provider to manage IT services.

PRINCE2

The standard UK government methodology for project management. See www.ogc.gov.uk/prince2/ for more information.

priority

A category used to identify the relative importance of an incident, problem or change. Priority is based on impact and urgency, and is used to identify required times for actions to be taken, e.g. the service level agreement may state that priority2 incidents must be resolved within 12 hours.

problem

A cause of one or more incidents. The cause is not usually known at the time a problem record is created, and the problem management process is responsible for further investigation.

problem management

The process responsible for managing the lifecycle of all problems. The primary objectives of problem management are to prevent incidents from happening, and to minimize the impact of incidents that cannot be prevented.

process

A structured set of activities designed to accomplish a specific objective. A process takes one or more defined inputs and turns them into defined outputs. A process may include any of the roles, responsibilities, tools and management controls required to reliably deliver the outputs. A process may define policies, standards, guidelines, activities, and work instructions if they are needed.

process control

The activity of planning and regulating a process, with the objective of performing the process in an effective, efficient and consistent manner.

programme

A number of projects and activities that are planned and managed together to achieve an overall set of related objectives and other outcomes.

provider

The organization concerned with the provision of ICT services.

release

A collection of hardware, software, documentation, processes or other components required to implement one or more approved changes to IT services. The contents of each release are managed, tested and deployed as a single entity.

release and deployment management

The process responsible for both release management and deployment.

request for change

A formal proposal for a change to be made. A request for change (RFC) includes details of the proposed change, and may be recorded on paper or electronically. The term RFC is often misused to mean a change record, or the change itself.

resolution

Action taken to repair the root cause of an incident or problem, or to implement a workaround. In ISO/IEC 20000, resolution processes is the process group that includes incident and problem management.

resources

A generic term that includes IT infrastructure, people, money or anything else that might help to deliver an IT service. Resources are considered to be assets of an organization.

return on investment

A measurement of the expected benefit of an investment. In the simplest sense it is the net profit of an investment divided by the net worth of the assets invested.

risk

A possible event that could cause harm or loss, or affect the ability to achieve objectives. A risk is measured by the probability of a threat, the vulnerability of the asset to that threat, and the impact it would have if it occurred.

risk management

The process responsible for identifying, assessing and controlling risks.

role

A set of responsibilities, activities and authorities granted to a person or team. A role is defined in a process. One person or team may have multiple roles, for example the roles of configuration manager and change manager may be carried out by a single person.

SAM

See software asset management.

SAM database

A database set containing all of the necessary information to support the effective operation of all SAM processes and the management of all software assets. It could form part of an overall configuration management system.

security management

Synonym for information security management.

security manager

The security manager is responsible for the security management process in the service provider organization. The person is responsible for fulfilling the security demands as specified in the service level agreement, either directly or through delegation by the service level manager. The security officer and the security manager work closely together.

service

A means of delivering value to customers by facilitating outcomes that customers want to achieve without the ownership of specific costs and risks.

service catalogue

A database or structured document with information about all live IT services, including those available for deployment. The service catalogue is the only part of the service portfolio published to customers, and is used to support the sale and delivery of IT services. The service catalogue includes information about deliverables, prices, contact points, ordering and request processes.

service desk

The single point of contact between the service provider and users. A typical service desk manages incidents and service requests, and also handles communication with the users.

service improvement plan

A formal plan to implement improvements to a process or IT service.

service knowledge management system

A set of tools and databases that are used to manage knowledge and information. The SKMS includes the configuration management system, as well as other tools and databases. The SKMS stores, manages, updates and presents all information that an IT service provider needs to manage the full lifecycle of IT services.

service level

Measured and reported achievement against one or more service level targets. The term service level is sometimes used informally to mean service level target.

service level agreement

An agreement between an IT service provider and a customer. The service level agreement (SLA) describes the IT service, documents service level targets, and specifies the responsibilities of the IT service provider and the customer. A single SLA may cover multiple IT services or multiple customers. See operational level agreement.

service level management

The process responsible for negotiating service level agreements, and ensuring that these are met. Service level management (SLM) is responsible for ensuring that all IT service management processes, operational level agreements, and underpinning contracts, are appropriate for the agreed service level targets. SLM monitors and reports on service levels, and holds regular customer reviews.

service level requirement

A customer requirement for an aspect of an IT service. Service level requirements (SLRs) are based on business objectives and are used to negotiate agreed service level targets.

service management

Service management is a set of specialized organizational capabilities for providing value to customers in the form of services.

service performance achievement

The actual service levels delivered by the ICT organization to a customer within a defined lifespan.

service provider

An organization supplying services to one or more internal customers or external customers. Service provider is often used as an abbreviation for IT service provider.

service request

A request from a user for information or advice, for a standard change or for access to an IT service, e.g. to reset a password, or to provide standard IT services for a new user. Service requests are usually handled by a service desk, and do not require submitting a request for change.

software asset management

All of the infrastructure and processes necessary for the effective management, control and protection of the software assets within an organization, throughout all stages of their lifecycle.

software configuration item

As 'configuration item', excluding hardware and services.

software library

A controlled collection of software configuration items designated to keep those with like status and type together and segregated from unlike, to aid in development, operation and maintenance.

stakeholder

All people who have an interest in an organization, project, IT service etc. Stakeholders may be interested in the activities, targets, resources or deliverables. Stakeholders include customers, partners, employees, shareholders, owners.

statement of requirements

A document containing all requirements for a product purchase, or a new or changed IT service.

system

A number of related things that work together to achieve an overall objective. For example:

- A computer system including hardware, software and applications
- A management system, including multiple processes that are planned and managed together, e.g. a quality management system
- A database management system or operating system that includes many software modules that are designed to perform a set of related functions.

third-party supplier

A person, group or business that is not part of the service level agreement for an IT service, but is required to ensure successful delivery of that IT service, e.g. a software supplier, a hardware maintenance company or a facilities department. Requirements for third parties are typically specified in underpinning contracts or operational level agreements.

threat

Anything that might exploit a vulnerability. Any potential cause of an incident can be considered to be a threat, e.g. a fire is a threat that could exploit the vulnerability of flammable floor coverings. This term is commonly used in information security management and IT service continuity management, but also applies to other areas such as problem and availability management.

total cost of ownership

A methodology used to help make investment decisions. The total cost of ownership assesses the full lifecycle cost of owning a configuration item, not just the initial cost or purchase price.

user

A person who uses the IT service on a day-to-day basis. Users are distinct from customers, as some customers do not use the IT service directly.

vendor-managed usage

The concept of vendors (i.e. software manufacturers) managing customers' use of licences, as opposed to the concept of customer-managed usage (CMU). See section 7.10 for a discussion of some vendor-managed technologies.

version

A version is used to identify a specific baseline of a configuration item. Versions typically use a naming convention that enables the sequence or date of each baseline to be identified, e.g. payroll application version 3 contains updated functionality from version 2.

version identifier

A version number, version date or version date and time stamp.

vulnerability

A weakness that could be exploited by a threat, e.g. an open firewall port, a password that is never changed or a flammable carpet. A missing control is also considered to be a vulnerability.

Index

Index

accommodation 13

acquisitions 8, 10

advisers 28

anti-piracy organizations 28, 87, 89, 90, 93

anti-virus software 57, 82

archiving 60

asset analysts 42

asset management 49

    asset control 50

    asset identification 50

    core asset management processes 49–51

    database management 50

    financial management 50–1

    hardware asset management 4

    IT asset management (ITAM) 4, 42

    status accounting 50

auditors 43, 87

audits 20, 40, 73, 89

    verification and audit 60–2

automation analysts 43

availability management 48, 49, 100–1

awareness 49, 70, 71, 116

backups 49, 111

British Computer Society Configuration Management
    Specialist Group 93

budgeting 102

build 55–7

business case 20, 31, 52, 145–6

    developing a vision and strategy 31–3

    documenting the business case 34

    investigating the issues 33–4

    selling the business case 35

business relationship management (BRM) 103

    internal business relationship management 64

Business Software Alliance (BSA) 7, 26, 28

capacity management 6, 77, 102

centralization 14, 39–40

    centralization or decentralization of SAM databases 40

Certificate in Software Asset Management Essentials 90

certification 89

    general procedural certifications 90

    personal certifications 90

    SAM and licence compliance certifications 89

change management 43, 102

client access licences 33, 112

COBIT 47, 97

    COBIT framework 105

    SAM and COBIT 104–7

communication 12

competence 15, 49

competitive advantage 10

compliance 6, 39, 58, 60

    employee compliance 150

    licensing compliance 62–3, 89

    security compliance 63

    verification and compliance processes 60–3

conferences 90

configuration librarians 42

configuration management system (CMS) 4, 6, 52, 93, 98, 100, 102, 129, 133
    ITIL use of the DML and CMS 99
configuration managers 42
Continual Service Improvement 101
    Continual Service Improvement 3, 18–20
continuity management 48, 49, 101
continuous improvement 49, 58
contract law 25
contract management 64
    contract management tools 82
contracting 14, 15, 41
Control Objectives for Information and Related Technology *see* COBIT
control processes 101–2
copyright 25, 26
cost–benefit analysis 15, 52
cost-effectiveness 9, 32, 53, 54, 59, 70, 88
costs 12–13
counterfeits 25–6, 55, 115–16
Cox, George 5
critical success factors (CSFs) 14, 33, 70, 71, 72, 145
customer-managed usage (CMU) 113
customized software 11, 13

decentralization 10–11, 39, 40
decision making 10
definitive media library (DML) 50, 98–100, 102
demand management tools 82
demergers 8, 64, 65, 101
Deming cycle 72
deployment 40, 57–8
    deployment management tools 82
    release and deployment managers 43
    retirement of deployment, but not of licences 59

software deployment optimization 58
software over-deployment 8–9
depreciation 9, 49, 50
design 53
directors 3, 48
    directors with legal responsibility 42
discovery tools 60–2, 79–80, 93
    ability to summarize meaningfully 80
    method and reliability of software identification 79–80
    networked versus non-networked use 79
discovery tools: platform 79
distributors 27
documentation 53, 71
    document management systems 79
    guidance documentation 136
    source documentation 134–5
    working documentation 135–6
downsizing 65–6

efficiency and effectiveness 6, 58–9
employees 7, 10, 12, 14, 25, 31, 32, 58, 63
    compliance with hardware/software policy 150
end-user licence agreement (EULA) 114, 117
end-users 9, 28, 65, 90
    end-user support 12
evaluation 53
event management 100

Federation Against Software Theft (FAST) 7, 28
financial analysis 146
financial exposure 7, 8, 23, 65, 117, 119
financial management 18, 32, 49, 50–1, 97, 98, 101
fire 49, 119
freeware 115

hard-disk loading 26
hardware 149–50
   hardware asset management 4
   hardware costs 9
   hardware dongles 83
   hardware inventory 136
   hardware retirement 59
high-volume licensing 114
HP 107
human resources (HR) 14

IBM 107
ICT 3, 6, 12, 34, 57
ICT infrastructure 9
ICT management 10, 41
   decentralization 11, 39
ICT planning 39
ICT research 93
implementation 13–14, 14–16, 20, 69
   getting there 70–2
   preparation 69–70
   proving you are staying there 72–3
   staying there 72
incident management 100
industry associations 87, 90
information and communications technologies see ICT
information security management 7, 15, 101
information technology infrastructure library see ITIL
information technology see IT
installation 23, 25, 26, 40
   installation security tools 82
   outsourcing 65
installed software 12
   installed software inventory 133–4
interfaces 13

International Organization for Standardization (ISO) 28
inventories 15, 133–4
   asset inventory tools 79
   downsizing 65–6
   software licence inventory 129–33
ISO 9000 3
ISO/IEC 19770 3, 28, 47, 89, 90, 103–4
ISO/IEC 20000 3, 20, 47, 97, 123
   SAM and ISO/IEC 20000 101–3
ISO/IEC 9001 90
IT 3
IT asset management (ITAM) 4, 42
IT service continuity management (ITSCM) 48, 49, 101
ITIL 3–4, 6, 28, 47, 48, 93, 97, 123
   how SAM maps to ITIL 16–20
   ITIL use of the DML and CMS 99
   relationship between SAM and the ITIL framework 17
   SAM and ITIL 16–20, 97–101

key performance indicators (KPIs) 14, 33, 34, 49, 64, 70, 71, 72, 145

legal advice/council 43
legal exposure 7, 24–6
legal requirements 12
licences 111
   corrective licences 13
   duration 112
   effective licences 118
   end-user type 113
   implementing physical management system 119
   licence management responsibility 113
   measure of usage 112–13
   physical management 117–19
   sales channels 114–15

licensing 7, 8, 20, 111
  basic types of licence 112–14
  corrective licences 13
  counterfeits 25–6, 115–16
  historical purchase records and effective licensing 91–2
  internal licensing support 9
  lack of clarity about the supply of licences 25
  licence management tools 81
  licensing advice 91
  licensing compliance 62–3
  licensing keys 83
  physical management of software licences 117–19
  proof of licence 116–17
  risks 23–4
  software licence inventory 129–33
  software licence variation 12
  software licensing for partially owned subsidiaries 119
  software licensing for sub-contractors/agents 119
  types of licence by sales channel 114–15
  verification of authenticity of licences 62
  when licences are required 111
lifecycle 4, 18, 20, 23, 49, 50
  application lifecycle 51, 52
  operation 58
  retirement 59–60
locked licences 114
logistics processes 48
  build 55–7
  deployment 57–8
  design 53
  evaluation 53
  operation 58
  optimization 58–9
  procurement 53–5

requirements definition 51–3
  retirement 59–60
low-volume licensing 114

management sponsors 42
management tool analysts 43
marketing 10
media 71, 118, 136
  definitive media library (DML) 50, 98–100, 102
mergers 8, 10, 65, 101
metering 83
metering tools 80–1
metrics 16, 34, 47, 49, 58, 64, 70, 71, 72, 73, 80, 134
Microsoft 107

National Audit Office 15–16
  recommendations for purchasing and managing software licences 16
negotiating position 8
non-volume proof of licence 55
novation 66

Office of Government Commerce (OGC) 3, 16, 97
open-source software 115
operation 40, 58
  continuity of operations 6, 8
  unsupportable operations 8
optimization 58–9
organizations 3–4, 9
  need for SAM 4–5, 14
  organizational culture 10–11, 13, 31, 41, 42, 70, 71, 72, 77, 103
original equipment manufacturers (OEMs) 27, 28, 117, 131, 132
  licences 114, 118

OEM proof of licence 55
retirement 59, 60
outsourcing 11, 14, 64–5, 87, 88

partners 20, 87, 139
audits 89
certification 89–90
conferences and workshops 90
current purchase records 92–3
directories and assessments of SAM tools 93
historical purchase records and effective licensing 91–2
implementation assistance for SAM tools 93
importance criteria for potential SAM partners 139–42
licensing advice 91
outsourcing of SAM functions 88
relationship management processes 63–5
SAM consultancy 88
SAM guidance material 87–8
SAM tools 93
special considerations for reseller relationships 93–4
people 13, 20
performance targets 58
Plan–Do–Check–Act (PDCA) 20, 72
policies 6, 14–15, 48
Practitioner Certificate in Software Asset Management 90
preparation 69–70
PRINCE2 14
problems 10–12
problem management 100
problem resolution 9
procedures 6, 15, 48
processes 6, 20, 47–8, 71
core asset management processes 49–51
infrastructure processes 9

logistics processes 51–60
overall management processes 48–9
relationship management processes 63–5
special situations 65–6
verification and compliance processes 60–3
procurement 6, 7, 8, 11, 12, 15, 24, 25, 50, 64, 79, 94, 101, 103, 124, 146, 149
procurement management 14, 23, 41, 43, 98
procurement process 23, 40, 48, 53–5, 62, 88
procurement tools 16, 82–3
products 20
ensuring product authenticity 55
professional associations 87, 90
projects 13–14, 35, 71
proof of licence 116–17
checking receipt of proof of licence 55, 56
electronic confirmations 118
loss of proof of licences 23–4, 119
manuals 118–19
media 118
OEM operating system licences 118
processing 54–5
protection tools 82
public domain software 115
pull technology 9, 51, 57
purchase records 91–3
purchasing arrangements 9
push technologies 57

recommendations 14–15
National Audit Office recommendations 15–16
reconciliations 15, 98, 136
records 60–2
recycling 59–60

relationship management processes 63
  contract management 64
  internal business relationship management 64
  outsourcing 64–5
  supplier management 64
relationship processes 101, 102
release and deployment managers 43
release processes 101–2
reorganizations 65
reports 71
reputation 7
request fulfilment management 100
resellers 24, 28, 39, 87, 90
  counterfeits 115, 116
  current purchase records 92–3
  historical purchase records 92
  licensing advice 91
  special considerations for reseller relationships 93–4
  tools 93
resolution processes 101–2
responsibilities 11, 12, 14–15, 20, 41–2, 97
  licence management responsibility 113
  overall management responsibility 48
retail licensing 114
retirement 59
  archiving 60
  options for recycling 59–60
  retirement of deployment, but not of licences 59
return on investment (ROI) 31, 34, 50, 146
reviews 6, 20, 72, 73
risk 23, 71
  breach of terms and conditions 24
  downsizing 65–6
  incorrect reliance on resellers 24

loss of licences 24
loss of proof of licences 23–4
mergers, demergers and reorganizations 65
novation 66
risk assessment 48
risk management 7–8, 39–40
senior management 31
unlicensed software 23
roles 12, 20, 41–2
  complementary roles 42–3
  primary roles 42
roll-outs 7, 9, 74, 75

SAM 3, 4
  costs 12–13
  definition 4
  examples of savings made through SAM 32–3
  how SAM maps to ITIL 16–20
  implementation approaches 13–14
  ISO/IEC 19770 103–4
  ISO/IEC 20000 101–3
  minimum implementation recommendations 14–16
  NAO and generic recommendations for purchasing and managing software licences 16
  need for SAM 4–5
  objective 5
  outsourcing of SAM functions 88
  possible problems 10–12
  relationship between SAM and the ITIL framework 17
  SAM and COBIT 104–7
  SAM and ITIL 16–20, 97–101
  SAM benefits 7–10
  SAM consultants 43, 87, 88
  SAM guidance material 87–8
  SAM implementation 69

SAM principles 5–6

SAM process areas 47

SAM process owners/managers 42

SAM procurement process 54

SAM technology architecture 78

SAM verification and compliance processes 61

tools 93, 123–4, 124–5

world-class SAM 16

SAM databases 4, 6, 7, 20, 50

centralization or decentralization 40

guidance documentation 136

hardware inventory 136

installed software inventory 133–4

media 136

software licence inventory 129–33

source documentation 134–5

working documentation 135–6

Sarbanes-Oxley 4, 31, 48

savings 8, 9, 10, 13, 32, 33, 39, 41, 51, 58, 65, 91

secondary usage licences 114

security management 42–3

security breaches 7

security tools 82

senior management 3, 5, 11, 12, 13, 14

business case 31, 35

implementation 71

overall management responsibility 48

personal risk 31

serialized licences 114

service asset and configuration management (SACM) 6, 97, 98–100, 116

service asset managers 42

service delivery processes 101, 102

Service Design 100–1

Service Design 3, 18, 64, 65, 77, 82

service desk management 43, 100

service level agreements (SLAs) 11

service level management (SLM) 100

service level requirement 52, 58, 125

service management 4

Service Operation 98, 100

Service Operation 3, 18

service provider licensing 114

Service Strategy 101

Service Strategy 3, 15, 18

Service Transition 98, 100

Service Transition 3, 4, 18

shareware 115

skills 15

Software & Information Industry Association 28

software asset management *see* SAM

software assets 23–4

legal context 24–6

software asset managers 42

software industry supply chain 26–8

software manufacturers 26, 87

software over-deployment 8–9

software policy 6, 149

acknowledgement of hardware/software policy 150

sample policy on the use of hardware and software 149–50

software publishers 26

Software Publishers Association (SPA) 28

software vendors 26, 83, 87

solution provider licensing 114

sourcing 39, 101

stakeholders 33, 145, 146

standards 28

statement of requirements (SoR) 53, 123, 124, 125

status accounting 50
strategy 5–6, 15, 20, 31–3, 34
   strategic infrastructure planning 8
suite licences 114
Sun 107
supplier and contracts database (SCD) 64
supplier management 64, 101, 103

tax 9, 50–1
TCO (total cost of ownership) 15, 32, 34, 50
technical licence management 83
terms of reference (ToR) 53
token-activated licences 114
tools 13, 20, 71, 77–9
   asset inventory tools 79
   considerations in selecting SAM tools 123–4
   contract management tools 82
   demand management tools 82
   deployment management tools 82
   directories and assessments of SAM tools 93
   discovery tools 60–2, 79–80, 93
   implementation assistance for SAM tools 93
   licence management tools 81
   metering tools 80–1
   practical guidelines for the selection of SAM tools 124–5
   procurement tools 16, 82–3
   protection tools 82
   SAM technology architecture 78
   SAM tools 93
   security tools 82
trademark legislation 25
training 28, 49, 64, 70, 71, 87, 111, 124, 125
   training courses 90
Turnbull 4, 48

UK 3, 4, 28, 48
upgrades 7, 8, 9, 24, 52–3
   contract management 64
   licences 113, 118
   upgrade rights 91
USA 4, 48

vendor licence management technology 83
vendor-managed usage (VMU) 83, 113
verification 79, 81
   verification and audit 60–2
   verification and compliance processes 61
   verification of authenticity of licences 62
version control 42
vision 5–6, 14, 20, 31–3
volume proof of licence 55

workers' councils 12, 81
workload impacts 7
workshops 90
wrapper technology 83